PEARL ✣ A STUDY
IN SPIRITUAL DRYNESS

PEARL
A STUDY IN SPIRITUAL DRYNESS

By
SISTER M. MADELEVA

PHAETON PRESS
New York
1968

Originally Published 1925
Reprinted 1968

98668

Library of Congress Catalog Card Number: 68-59311
Published by PHAETON PRESS

TO
MY ASSISTANT
IN GRATITUDE

FOREWORD

Any one who engages even superficially in the study of medieval religious poetry becomes aware, almost at once, of a Catholic world so rich in imaginative and institutional teaching and practice that he cannot but covet for the successful prosecution of his studies a very deep and special knowledge of the life and discipline, particularly the community life and discipline, of the Church. Poems written by monks, nuns, and priests, and filled with phrases and symbols taken from the most homely and endearing, from the most laborious, the most intimate, the most sublime and sacred phases of their discipline, cannot but have had for the religious a very special savour and intensity. The idiom of the daily task and ever recurring struggle of personal adjustment, no less than the eloquence of Missal and Breviary, was caught up in the meditations, now evangelically importunate, now mystically serene, of this devout literature. The layman can gather only some faint suggestion of the intimacy and force of the associations that both familiar and

vii

sublime phrases started in the mind of a religious. By missing connotation, he misses much of imaginative and emotional effect. Words tend to become dry and monotonous, symbols empty and conventional.

But that also the essential meaning of a poem may be obscure to even the most learned of laymen has been proved, perhaps, by Sister Madeleva's study of the *Pearl*. Years ago, when she first read this poem, Sister Madeleva was struck by its congruity in many respects with the experiences of the life of a religious, for the Church has preserved through the centuries, almost without change, many of the customs, much of the routine, even the dialect, of the medieval religious community. Later study, especially in the direction of Catholic mysticism, and her creative participation in that lovely life of the spirit, only served to convince the author that the *Pearl* is to be interpreted mystically and symbolically in relation to one of the most important experiences of the inner life of a religious.

Such an interpretation is here placed before the public, and the author is to be congratulated upon having made a most valuable and definitive contribution to the study of this much discussed composition. The explication that hitherto has most generally obtained—that of an elegy upon the

death of a little daughter—seems peculiarly in-
ept, even absurd, in the light shed upon the spiritually autobiographic character of the work by the
sympathetic understanding of this daughter of the
Church. Any one who will read carefully what
the author has to say concerning the 144,000
virgins of the poem (vv. 781-872) will find it
exceedingly difficult to continue to adhere to the
elegiac interpretation, and uncommonly tempting
to accept at once this new symbolic reading. As
he goes further, temptation may well yield to
conviction, for, point by point, line by line, the
Pearl fits in most consistently with the present
explanation. And as, step by step, the poem is
thus brought home again to the wealth of spiritual
life in the religious community, it takes on, in my
opinion, an ever increasing significance and beauty.

BENJAMIN P. KURTZ.

ACKNOWLEDGMENT

The author wishes to thank the editor of *Pearl*, Sir Israel Gollancz, Litt.D., F.B.A., and the publishers, Chatto and Windus, for permission to embody quotations from their 1921 edition of the poem in this study. Sir Israel Gollancz's rendering of *The Pearl* is published, in America, by the Oxford University Press in the Mediæval Library.

AUTHOR'S NOTE

One does not come out of the discipline of
scholarly research without a very wholesome re-
spect for sources, original forms, first-hand material, and a sober sense of just the kind of support such evidence contributes to a theory, much
more, to a thesis. This interpretation of the
Pearl has been built on such sources and material. In its scholarly form, all citations appear
in the original, or in such translations as would
have been used at particular periods in question,
that is, as far as such copies exist or were pro-
curable.

On the advice of scholars interested in all fields
involved in this study, literature, criticism, philology, I have substituted the easier modern
forms for the splendid but often difficult Middle
English originals, and translations for the Syriac,
Latin, German, and French. What the work has
lost to precise scholarship by these concessions to
our linguistic limitations, it has gained, I trust,
in a homelier and more general understanding.

S. M. M.

CONTENTS

PEARL ✶ A STUDY IN SPIRITUAL DRYNESS

CHAPTER I

CRITICAL INTERPRETATIONS OF "PEARL"

In 1864 Richard Morris published in the first number of the *Early English Text Society Reprints* a prose rendering of *Pearl,* an alliterative poem in the Midland dialect of about 1370, found in a single manuscript (*Cotton Nero* A X, British Museum), with three other alliterative poems, *Sir Gawain and the Green Knight, Cleanness,* and *Patience.* The poem, appearing then for the first time in print, was reëdited and reprinted in 1869, in 1885, in 1896, and in 1901. Meanwhile, Sir Israel Gollancz had in 1891 published the poem in its original form with a modern, unrhymed rendering facing the Middle English text; which edition he reissued in 1921, together with Boccaccio's *Olympia.* His contribution *par excellence* he made in 1923 in his page by page facsimile edition of the poem. Between 1905 and 1907 five editions of the *Pearl* appeared; a line for line version in the meter of the original by Professor G. G. Coulton (London), modern versions by Professor C. G. Osgood (Princeton), Sophie Jewett (New York), and Marion Mead (Portland, Maine), and a rendering of the first half of the poem by Doctor S. Weir Mitchell (New York). Clearly, something more than a desultory interest attaches to this most perfect of Middle English poems.

For the past half century careful and devoted scholars have been busy with the *Pearl,* yet research has pretty generally come out by the same door wherein it went. Three problems have concerned critics chiefly: the author of the poem, its elegiac character, and its symbolism. Elaborate cases have been made out for Huchown, for the philosophical Strode, for Richard Rolle, and for an anonymous secular, unhappily married and the father of a two-year-old daughter whose death he laments in the poem. Hypothetical biographies have been supplied, revealing possible skeletons in the family closets and interpreting the whole poem in the light of this purely fictitious family history. The pages of mediæval romances and lapidaries have been scanned microscopically for references to pearls that could in the remotest way have a bearing upon this lovely jewel. All the while material close at hand has been overlooked, and an obvious interpretation neglected. It is the interpretation of the *Pearl* as an exposition of spiritual dryness or interior desolation—one of the most familiar of spiritual conditions—with the subsequent questionings, hopes, and resignation which normally grow out of it. Such an interpretation I shall make. I use for my text the 1921 edition of *Pearl*, by Professor Gollancz, and ignore for the moment all questions of poetic forms, dialect, sources, translations *per se*, considering only the meaning of the poem as one would read it either out of the precious old manuscript itself or from any of the prose or verse versions more easily available.

Boldly, I call the *Pearl* a spiritual autobiography, a study in dryness and interior desolation. In blazing this new trail I am not ignoring the more or less traveled roads mapped out by Professors Gollancz,[1] Osgood,[2] Brown,[3] Coulton,[4] Schofield,[5] and Garrett.[6] Indeed, a careful ex-

[1] Gollancz, *Encyclopedia Britannica*, Ed. XI, Vol. XXI, also Introduction to *Pearl*, Ed. 1921.
[2] C. G. Osgood, Introduction to *The Pearl*, London, 1906.
[3] C. Brown, *Publications of the Modern Language Association*, Vol. XIX, pp. 114-154.
[4] G. G. Coulton, *Modern Language Review*, Vol. 21, XXIV.
[5] W. H. Schofield, *Publications of the Modern Language Association*, Vol. XIX, pp. 154-215; Vol. XXIV, pp. 585-675.
[6] R. M. Garrett, *University of Washington Publications*, Vol. IV, No. 1, pp. 1-45.

ploration of each of these is an essential before
venturing upon my own. A summary of the poem
will serve as a starting point.

The author has lost a "perle plesaunte"—it
has slipped from him into the grass, he says. In
the weariness and sorrow of fruitless search he
falls asleep and dreams of a beautiful young girl
in whom he thinks he recognizes his pearl. She
explains to him that his pearl is not lost and
chides him for desiring its sensible possession.
She explains her marriage to the spotless Lamb,
the parable of the vineyard, the efficacy of grace,
the salvation and reward of baptized children
as compared with adults. She concludes with a
paraphrase of the fourteenth, twenty-first, and
twenty-second chapters of the Apocalypse, the
vision of the New Jerusalem. The poet reaches
the ecstatic climax of his dream when he beholds
his pearl, a "lyttle quene" in the company of the
Lamb Whom virgins alone can approach. Vision
can carry him no further. He wakes, shaken
with joy, "maddying." But, restrained by soberer
thought, he is resigned to the will of God; and
strengthened by Christ in the Blessed Sacrament,
he is content to wait His good pleasure and to
serve Him always.

Critics are practically unanimous in interpreting the poem as a tenderly allegorical elegy, turn-

ing upon the sorrow of a father for the death of his two-year-old daughter, Pearl, and ascribe it quite generally to the unknown author or authors of the other three poems found in the same manuscript with it. Doctor Morris has first claim to this theory, as he has to the earliest translation of the poem. He says in a prefatory note to his translation: "In . . . *The Pearl* the author evidently gives expression to his own sorrow for the loss of his infant child, a girl of two years old." Ten Brink accepts the interpretation without question and builds upon it this attractive but unjustifiable biography:

> The poet had married (his lord having, perhaps, given him a home of his own as a reward for faithful service). A child, a sweet girl, radiant in innocence, had blessed this union. The father concentrated all his affection upon the child, and so exclusively that we are led to believe the mother had not long survived her birth. The dearest ideals of the thoughtful poet were embodied in his daughter. But the pitiless hand of fate tore her away at the tenderest age. The poem describes the father's feelings at her death, and tells how he was comforted.[7]

Upon this structure of intense parental devotion, practically all subsequent interpretations of the poem rest.

---

[7] Ten Brink, *Early English Literature,* London, 1883, p. 348.

Coming to the findings of particular scholars, we may well begin with Professor Gollancz. In his article on *Pearl* in the *Encyclopedia Britannica* as well as in his introductions to his various editions of the poem, he consistently advances the conventional interpretation—the father and daughter theory. While setting Boccaccio's *Olympia* side by side with *Pearl* in a single volume and disclaiming the influence of the former on the latter, he is curiously unconscious of the significance of his own statement, as well as of the difference in their spirit and treatment. This is almost inevitable, however, considering how much of the narrowly elegiac he reads into the English poem.

This is less important than his manner of editing the poem. Here he is unfair to himself and misleading to his readers. Beginning with the assumption that the *Pearl* is a maiden, he capitalizes the word in appropriate places throughout his text to support this assumption. In the first twelve lines, the word occurs four times; three times he capitalizes it, and once he spells it as a common noun. In the original text which faces his own rendering, he omits the capitals entirely except in lines 411, 745, 902, and 1192. Obviously, his manner of printing the word is arbitrary. Worse than that, it is unauthorized, for the manu-

script itself, a facsimile of which Professor Gollancz brought out in 1923, nowhere shows a
capitalization of *Pearl,* except when it stands at
the beginning of the line. One might try capi-
talizing the word *daisy* in Wordsworth's poems to
a daisy, or *lily* and *rose* in "Maud" and see what
hypothetical supplements to the biographies of the
authors could be made plausible by the alterations.
Also, his use of the possessive adjective "my"
to modify *Pearl,* as in lines 8 and 41, changes
the meaning of the lines as they stand in the
manuscript, and while it confirms perceptibly his
own interpretation, gets decidedly between the
reader and the meaning of the poet. The lines:

> So smal, so smothe her sydez were
> Quere-so-ever I jugged gemmez gaye.
> I sette hyr sengeley in syng(u)l(e)re

and

> I dewyne, for-do(k)ked of luf-daungere
> Of that pryuy perle wyth-outen spot.

as they stand in the original do not give one the
personal and possessive sense of Professor Gollancz's:

> I placed my Pearl apart, supreme,

and

> I pine, by Severing Love despoil'd
> Of Pearl mine own, without a spot.

and one feels that these elements are contributed by the translator rather than by the poet. Supposing that the poet had no *person* in mind when he apostrophized "Perle plesaunte," the lovely freedom of the rendering becomes an imposition. This supposition will be advanced presently, when it will be imperative to insist upon fidelity to the original.

Professor Osgood, in an excellently careful and complete introduction to his edition of 1906, accepts the "father and daughter" theory. "The poem is first of all," he says, "an elegy." [8] Then, assuming that the same man wrote all four poems in the Cotton Manuscript, he bases a hypothetical biography of the *Pearl* poet on evidences found in the other three. For instance, he states that the author could not have been an ecclesiastic because of his glorification of marriage in *Cleanness,* a conclusion sufficiently astounding and ungrounded to give one pause. It should have occurred to him that matrimony is, in Catholic doctrine which obtains here, as true a sacrament as Holy Orders, instituted before it and, biologically at least, essential to it; that the Church is the prime promoter of matrimony; that ecclesiastics are its only indispensable witnesses and that

---

[8] C. G. Osgood, Introduction to *Pearl,* London, 1906, Vol. XXVIII.

not a few of them have lost their heads in its defense. He assumes that the poet has known both the luxury and the temptations of Sir Gawain, the prowess and the splendor of the bravest knight in Arthur's court, as well as the unholy allurements that, in the poem, the world, the flesh, and the devil contrive against such a one. He attributes to him, in theory at least, all the personal experiences reflected in the three companion poems; he grafts upon him the lives of three other possible men, for whose existence he offers no substantial proof. His carefully erected and elaborately unsupported structure topples because it is built on less than sand. Which would be of no great moment, except that Professor Osgood's understanding of the poem rests on these assumptions. An impersonal study of the four poems discovers at least as many differences as resemblances. A common scribe joined them together —a glowing example of the responsibility of the irresponsible—but I am inclined to think that if the four were separated and bound promiscuously among collections of Early English texts, not even the overeagerness of research would put them together again. Professor Osgood's contribution, while pleasant and sincere, is, for scholarly purposes, gratuitous. Critics five hundred years from now will not be justified in building up a biography of Wordsworth on the experiences of Coleridge, simply because the poems of the two are deliberately bound up together, and show certain identities of interest, influence, and even expression.

With something of a trail-blazer's instinct, Professor Schofield strikes boldly out and away from this and other beaten paths, and in his "Symbolism, Allegory and Autobiography in the *Pearl*," [9] points the way to a new and what seems to me a correct interpretation of the poem. He rejects the "father and daughter" theory entirely. He says:

The opening stanza contains no mention whatever of the Maiden Pearl. . . . The statements in these lines are only to be taken literally . . . it is evident that, beginning themselves with the wrong impression that the girl Pearl is mentioned at the very start of the poem, critics . . . have lost sight of the author's artistic plan in the structure of the work. . . . The poem . . . gives us no warrant for saying that the author was ever married at all, or ever had a child other than one of his own imagination. . . . Study the poem with the utmost care and one is bound to admit that the author does not reveal what one can be sure is a single "personal" experience of his natural life—even less than the almost contemporary author of *The Imitation of Christ,* who had so much in common with our poet.

---

[9] W. H. Schofield, *Publications of the Modern Language Association*, Vol. XXIV, pp. 584-675.

This all but concluding sentence of his study is, it seems to me, the most significant statement in it. However, Professor Schofield appears to be half afraid of his own temerity, and finding himself in strange and unfamiliar places, returns to the ground of the old criticisms. He starts down at least two new, true paths but does not follow either. He seems to distrust his own statement that the poet never had a daughter, and weakens the significance of his speech by the apology that perhaps the poet is expressing a desire for a relationship that he never realized. Which is perfectly irrelevant as a conclusion and perfectly lifeless as an interpretation—a complete anticlimax to all that his luminous suggestions promised.

One wishes sincerely and repeatedly that Professor Schofield had matched his brilliance in finding clues with perseverance in following them. Failure to do this has taken the vitality out of two other half-made points in the article under discussion. He says (p. 627) :

The author of *Pearl* has peopled paradise with none but maidens. He mentions no apostles, no martyrs or confessors, but only virgins. Yet he holds out the hope that we may all gain the rewards of Heaven.

By which he seems to imply that these inhabitants of paradise are exclusively female in sex.

If so, he is mistaken in the meaning and use of the words "virgin" and "maiden." A virgin, always in Catholic theology and certainly at the time that *Pearl* was written, meant a person bound by the vow of chastity or living in that state, without reference to sex. "Maiden" had the same freedom from sex signification, though it has been more apt in losing it. The gender of the "maiden knight" of this period suffers no confusion by reason of the adjective. One understands quite perfectly King Arthur's speech to Guinevere, "I am a maiden but for you." Moreover, the word "vergyne" rather than "maydenne" is used in the line which describes the heavenly company of the *Pearl,* thus obviating any possible limitation. In heaven the necessity of sex will have ceased while the two categories of married and virgin souls, as determined by human existence, will remain. The fact that the poet has put none but virgins into the heaven of his vision is deeply significant; it was the heaven of his dreams, his hopes, and his impassioned desires, which can only mean that he was living a life of which that would be the ultimate and endless fulfillment. He must have been a religious or at least unmarried. No man, married in fact or in desire, would be moved to express with such ardor as one finds in the poem, his personal longing for a condition that he had willingly and irrevocably foregone. Which is a conclusion that Professor Schofield did not follow to its obvious end.

With the same facility for brilliant conjecture, he insists that *purity* is first and foremost the theme of *Pearl*—my own first guess—and somewhat later, in discussing the poet, says, "I have myself no doubt about his authorship of *Cleanness* and *Patience*." In view of the fact that purity is the expressed and repeated theme of *Cleanness*, it would seem that the very great difference in matter and manner between it and *Pearl* would disturb his belief either in their common authorship or their identity of subject.

His earlier article, "The Nature and Fabric of the *Pearl*," [10] must be considered in connection with Professor Coulton's "In Defense of *Pearl*,"[11] a destructive criticism of Professor Schofield's less scholarly contribution. Against his statement that an ecclesiastic could have none but illegitimate children, Professor Coulton sets Sir Thomas More with disconcerting directness; Beatrice he cites as a case parallel to Pearl in which the leading lady is not described and in which behavior

[10] *Publications of the Modern Language Association,* Vol. XIX, pp. 154-215.
[11] *Modern Language Review,* Vol. II, pp. 39-43.

in heaven is not entirely consistent with age and
condition on earth. It was on the absence of
personal description and the unchildlike quality
of Pearl's converse that Professor Schofield rested
his argument against her reality as a child; and
on the fact that ecclesiastics could not lawfully
have children that he postulates illegitimacy, in
case a real child was the subject of the poem.
One feels that he merited some such hard-hearted
reprimand for his amiable acceptance of Professor Carleton Brown's ex-cathedra statement
that the author was an ecclesiastic.[12] Of which
more presently. Meanwhile Professor Coulton
has not faced the fact that Beatrice's attitude to
Dante throughout his supernatural pilgrimage is
entirely consistent with his relation to her on
earth; while Pearl, granted that she is a daughter,
speaks as no father could imagine his child, grown
to womanhood, would do. The question is of no
particular importance, but I put it to fathers of
baby girls—their relations to them have not
changed too much for argument during the centuries. Also Professor Coulton says that "our
rude forefathers . . . took Pearl as an elegy."
I should welcome evidence in proof of the statement. Neither criticism nor interpretation of the

---

[12] C. Brown, *Publications of the Modern Language Association,* Vol. XIX, pp. 115-153.

poem goes back further than the nineteenth century. Mary Segar has hazarded some such guess [13] but she offers it only as a probability *contrary* to the usual opinion. As to general interpretation, Professor Coulton enlists with the body of scholarly traditionalists in regarding Pearl as a real child and the poet her bereaved and stricken father.

So, too, does Professor Carleton Brown; though in his article, "The Author of the *Pearl*, Considered in the Light of His Theological Opinions," [14] he scampers blithely about in the fields of the Post-Nicene Fathers, Scholastic theology, and Pelagianism in its various degrees for forty pages, to come to the most unexpected conclusion that *Pearl* "is a most interesting and remarkable anticipation of sixteenth century Protestantism." Why not of sixteenth century Catholicism?—having for its essence almost, definitions of grace and its dispensations, the heaven of infants and of virgins which have not been identified with Protestantism in any century and have consistently been taught by the Catholic Church in all centuries. Professor Brown's unhappy gift of *non*

---

[13] "Alexandria and the Mystical Writings of the Middle Ages," *Catholic World*, August, 1924.

[14] *Publications of the Modern Language Association*, Vol. XIX, pp. 115-153.

sequitur pursues and betrays him still further. After laboring through Saints Jerome, Augustine, Gregory, Bonaventure, Thomas Aquinas, Duns Scotus, Peter Lombard, and Bradwardine in order to explain the teachings of the *Pearl* poet, he comes to the utterly unexpected and irrelevant conclusion that the author's purpose was "evangelical rather than ecclesiastical." It would be illuminating in this case to know just what he understands by each of his terms, and which of a number of possible distinctions between the words he has in mind.

Professor Brown scents heresy and incipient Protestantism in the fact that "Holy Church is not once mentioned" in the poem, that "in the picture of the New Jerusalem hierarchical dignitaries have no place." One finds the same omissions in the *Imitation of Christ,* the *Revelations of Blessed Juliana of Norwich,* the *Form of Perfect Living,* to mention only a few contemporary books of orthodox Catholicism in the same field. In fact, one finds these subjects appearing much more commonly in semi-heretical than in orthodox books of a literary character, at this period and down to the present hour, as witness, *The Vision of Piers Plowman, The Faery Queene, Pilgrim's Progress.* Why the absence of church dignitaries should constitute either an omission or an embryonic heresy is hard to see. Their conspicuous appearance in Dante's vision of the next world (*Inferno*, Canto XIX) has never been taken seriously as an argument either for or against his orthodoxy. "Still more significant," continues Professor Brown, "is our author's disregard for patristic authority and tradition. We miss . . . 'as seynt Austin saith.'" But he need not miss it; it is lacking in much of the religious and most of the mystical writing of the time. Especially is it absent from poetry. And, if Professor Brown has read his theology well, he will remember that the doctrine of infant baptism, which loons so large in the poem, rests entirely on tradition and patristic authority. Since *Pearl* assumed neither the scope of an epic nor the purposes of a theology, these omissions are indications rather of the poet's artistic sense of congruity and unity than his subdued resentment to Church authority.

But the tireless dogmatic search that Professor Brown pursues to so little purpose here, he turns to fine account in his criticism of Mr. Garrett's article on the subject.[15] According to it, the *Pearl* is one of the great fourteenth century tributes to the Holy Eucharist, among which St. Thomas Aquinas' *Mass of Corpus Christi*, the *Opus Maius*

[15] R. M. Garrett, *"Pearl,* An Interpretation," *University of Washington Publications,* Vol. IV, pp. 1-45.

of Roger Bacon and the *Legend of the Holy Grail*
hold first place. The interpretation is intricately
symbolic; Mr. Garrett reads the poem against
a background of Catholic doctrine and devotion:
the Holy Eucharist, the Communion of Saints, and
the Adoration of the Lamb. While the first two
are subjects of Catholic faith and devotion immediately recognizable, the last is a violent excerpt from the Canon of the Mass, grotesque and
quite unprecedented. Catholic devotion has frequently focused on the Sacred Heart, the Holy
Infancy, on the Holy Cross of Christ as aspects
of His life and love, but apart from its distinct
and august place in the Mass, the Agnus Dei, the
Adoration of the Lamb has, I think, never been a
form of Catholic devotion, nor is it, indeed, the
aspect under which Christ is worshiped in the
Mass. The word "Lamb" is used as a symbol
of a victim offered in sacrifice, a fulfillment of the
Jewish Paschal lamb, which meaning, applied to
the *Pearl,* is quite incongruous.

The only other aspect under which the Lamb
appears in forms of Catholic piety is the Agnus
Dei, a very common sacramental, made from the
wax of the Paschal candle, a symbol of sacrifice,
and used for protection against storm, flood, and
pestilence, and in child-birth. Agnus Deis were so
well known in Mediæval England as to be for-

bidden by the penal laws under Elizabeth as
"popish trumperies." [16] So that, in thinking together the Agnus Dei of the Mass with the Lamb
of the *Pearl,* Mr. Garrett is, for purposes of his
own hypothesis, forcing the two to fit into a relation that did not exist, rather than pointing out
the happy expression of one that did.

I should extend the same criticism to his statement that the structure of the poem conforms
roughly to that of the Mass. I have attended
Mass every day for twenty years, and have studied
the *Pearl* during at least half that time, and now
only by a distortion of both can I force their
technic into lines of any significant similarity. If
the two "conform roughly," it is so very roughly
that research need not be bothered by the resemblance. The great divisions of the Mass are not,
as Mr. Garrett states, the Pro-Anaphora, Canon,
Agnus Dei, and Adoration; they are the Offertory,
the Consecration, and the Communion, the last
two of which are included in the Canon of the
Mass. So, by making the poem fit into a wrong
structure, he has hardly proved a genuine resemblance. The critic draws his terminology from
Eastern liturgies which have never been used in the
Western Church and which would have been quite

---

16 "Agnus Dei," *Catholic Encyclopedia,* Vol. I, p. 220.

unfamiliar to the mediæval monk, much more the mediæval secular. The Agnus Dei and Adoration, whatever Mr. Garrett may mean by that, are not separate from the Canon of the Mass, as his division indicates; but, with the Consecration, Elevation, and Communion, constitute it.

As for the far-fetched symbolism of the Eucharist discovered in the Pearl of the New Testament, the Eucharist as a Pearl, and Christ as the Pearl of Great Price, I think that Professor Brown has shown excellently well and beyond need of further discussion the impossibility of Mr. Garrett's interpretation, beautiful as it is;[17] and at the same time, has disposed of Mr. Northrup's complacent acquiescence to it.[18] One might supplement it by this further note; Mr. Garrett makes *roundness* a point of resemblance between a pearl and the consecrated Host. It is actually a point of difference; one is spherical and the other is circular in form. Also, shape has nothing to do with the nature or essence of the Holy Eucharist, while it has with a pearl. Moreover, in the Eastern Greek rite, on which Mr. Garrett has based his other parallels, the sacrificial Host used in exposition for the adoration of the faith-

---

[17] C. Brown, *Modern Language Notes,* Vol. 34, p. 42.
[18] C. S. Northrup, *Journal of English and Germanic Philology,* Vol. 20, p. 288.

ful is not round, but square, to express mystically
that by the Sacrifice of the Cross redemption is
granted to the four quarters of the globe.[19] Adherence to the usages in this rite destroys his
parallel between the round Host and the round
pearl, however it may fit into his theory of the
spotless Lamb. The only possible reference of
the poem to the Holy Eucharist that might be
pushed, Mr. Garrett has missed. It is the fishes
that one finds in three of the four illustrations
in the book. From the days of the apostles to
the coat of arms of the present bishop of Sacra-
mento, the fish has been used to symbolize the
Blessed Sacrament. Here, however, it is so naïve
a confession of the limitations of the artist that
we understand the fishes to identify the place
they occupy in the pictures as a river, and do not
press them into any misguided service of symbolism.

This, then, concludes a history of the critical
interpretations of the *Pearl,* with the disposition
of accidental points by the way. Manuals and
histories of English Literature are unanimous in
accepting the "father and daughter" theory agreed
upon by the body of critics, Professor Schofield
excepted, and in regarding the poem as one of

---

[19] "Host," *Catholic Encyclopedia,* Vol. VII, pp. 494, 495.

the great elegies in the language. I propose to set aside completely this theory, to interpret the poem as a purely subjective study in spiritual dryness, interior desolation, a lament for the loss of the sensible sweetness of God and as such only elegiac, one of the great spiritual autobiographies, comparable in part to the book of Job, in English literature.

CHAPTER II

AN EXPOSITION OF SPIRITUAL DRYNESS

As introductory to such an interpretation some explanation of the spiritual life will be helpful. The term "natural or physical life" is perfectly familiar to all of us; we understand that it pertains to the body, its growth, development, perfection, its health or disease, its comfort or discomfort. By substituting *soul* for *body* we can arrive at a very adequate idea of what is meant by the "spiritual life." It is concerned entirely with the soul, its perfection and the means thereto, its well-being, and its particular ills. It is the development of this spiritual life that every person has in mind who consecrates himself to God in a religious order or the secular priesthood. His ultimate goal is always God; his immediate end is the perfection of his own soul. Now, as soon as an athlete begins to train for some particular contest, he immediately discovers, not only a host of unsuspected exercises to be performed, but also many actual dangers to his physical fitness, of which, in a less specialized condition, he was en-

23

tirely unconscious. The spiritual athlete makes
much the same discoveries. He had thought that
the religious life was a state of security and rest;
he finds that it is a series of exercises, conflicts
amounting at times to a very violent internal war-
fare. He has constantly to deny himself, to exercise himself, to hold himself in readiness. Quite
inevitably, he reacts in mind as well as in soul to
all these things. At times he is alert, eager, fit,
in excellent condition, and overjoyed at the consciousness of it. He is in love with the race for
perfection; he welcomes every difficulty that it
involves. The thought of the Prize and the ex-
hilaration of the struggle stimulate and captivate
his soul. God is almost a sensible Reality to him,
and he literally feels the keenest delight in serving
Him. He can make his meditations without difficulty, can say his prayers without distractions.
Seculars commonly consider this the chronic state
of the religious, but they could not be more mistaken. This condition is known in religious parlance as spiritual joy, sweetness, or consolation.
It is not a necessary condition for perfection, but
a very encouraging one, and is a common experience among young aspirants. Their own natural
enthusiasm contributes much to it; God, knowing
their need of encouragement, is generous in giving
this grace in abundance at the beginning of the

religious life. It is not to be relied or depended on, however, any more than is the physical athlete's own natural exuberance. It is his endurance which will count in the long run.

It was in this spirit of interior consolation that David sang: "I will go unto the altar of God, to God Who giveth joy to my youth," and that St. Francis of Assisi, more than twenty centuries later, burst into song as he set out from his father's house on his tremendous and sudden race to God. The reality of this spiritual condition is vouched for by all spiritual writers, from the Fathers of the desert to masters of the interior life whose manuscripts on the subject are yet in the making. One reads in *The Paradise or Garden of the Holy Fathers*:[20] "There are two things peculiar to the cell; the one warmeth and setteth on fire, and the other giveth light and rejoicing." Cassian advises religious to be "ever joyful with an insight into things eternal and future." [21] One may remark here that Cassian, throughout his *Institutes,* uses the figure of "the athlete of Christ" (pp. 237*ff*., 267) to describe one being

---

[20] Compiled by Athanasius, Palladius, St. Jerome and others, translated out of the Syriac by Ernest A. W. Budge, London, 1907.

[21] The Institutes of John Cassian, *Nicene and Post-Nicene Fathers,* Vol. XI, p. 266, translated under the editorial supervision of Philip Schaff and Henry Wace, New York, 1894.

trained in the spiritual life. One finds in the
Ancren Riwle a more personal expression of the
same experience:

If thou wilt be such, let no man see thy countenance,
nor blithely hear thy speech; but keep them both for
Christ, for thy beloved spouse, as he bade thee before;
as thou desirest that thy speech may seem sweet to him,
and thy countenance fair, and to have him to be thy
beloved who is a thousand times brighter than the sun.[22]

Juliana of Norwich is inimitable in the quaint
simplicity of her expression: "Thus saw I that
God is our very peace, and He is our sure Keeper
when we are ourselves in unpeace, and He con-
tinually worketh to bring us into endless peace."
"Flee we to our Lord, and we shall be comforted,
touch Him and we shall be made clean, cleave
we to Him and we shall be sure, and safe from all
manner of peril." [23]   Her great contemporary,
Richard Rolle, desired in *The Form of Perfect
Living* that "the sweetness of His [God's] grace
be our comfort and our solace in weal and woe.
If thou lovest him much," he continues, "great
joy and sweetness and burning thou feelest in His

---

[22] *Ancren Riwle,* edited and translated from the semi-Saxon
Ms. of the 13th century by James Morton, London, 1853, pp.
98-100.

[23] Juliana of Norwich, *Revelations of Divine Love,* London,
1923, pp. 104-189.

love, that is thy comfort and strength night and day." [24] From these examples it is evident that the condition of interior joy or consolation was entirely familiar to persons of deep religious feeling or to those aspiring to perfection, as far back as we have records of such aspirations in the Christian era, and certainly within the century that the *Pearl* was written.

But as a person advances in the spiritual life, he experiences frequent withdrawals of this sensible sweetness. The effect upon him is immediate. At first he is bewildered, desolate, downcast, and discouraged. He feels that God has abandoned him, and, left to himself, he knows that he can do nothing. He casts about for the causes of his apparent desertion and usually locates it in his own unworthiness. This humility is the first fruit of his trial though it is hard for him to realize it at the time. He fears that he is failing in his pursuit of perfection and is more disturbed in heart and soul than he would be over any loss or sorrow whatever. This condition is known as aridity, spiritual dryness, or interior desolation. It is exceedingly profitable to the soul, because during such a trial one discovers just how substantial one's virtue is, or as St. Francis de Sales

[24] *The Form of Perfect Living,* rendered into Modern English by G. E. Hodgson, London, 1910, p. 9.

puts it, whether one loves the God of consolations or only the consolations of God. This state of soul may be as transient as a passing feeling or, as in the cases of any number of saints, it may last for months. St. Teresa is a conspicuous example. She tells us in her autobiography:

> I suffered at times—and even still, though not so often, the most grievous spiritual trials. I forgot all the mercies our Lord has shown me, and remembered them only as a dream. . . . That it is his (the devil's) work is clear from the restlessness and discomfort with which it begins, and the trouble it causes the soul while it lasts; from the obscurity and distress, the aridity and indisposition for prayer and for every good work, which it produces. . . . What I understood by it is this: that it is our Lord's pleasure to give him (the devil) leave and license, as he gave him of old to tempt Job. The trial continued one, two, and even three weeks. It is impossible to describe the sufferings of the soul in this state. It goes about in quest of relief, and God suffers it to find none.[25]

It is perhaps the commonest of all trials in the spiritual life and one on which almost every spiritual writer has had something to say. An old French manuscript, intended for private use, offers this excellent summary:

> Generally speaking, interior trials do not come in the first state of the spiritual life. In the beginning, God

[25] *St. Teresa, An Autobiography,* edited by John J. Burke, New York, 1911, pp. 220-222.

ordinarily draws souls by means of sensible consolations.
. . . But scarcely is that soul well established like a true
dove in the cleft of the rock . . . than her Lord requires
her to catch the little foxes and to destroy those thousand
little passions which will persist in springing up again.

It is impossible that trials of this kind should not appear very early in the spiritual life, and they are a sign
of the real advancement of a soul which our Lord is
following up with special care.[26]

One can trace the history of spiritual desolation with the same continuity as the more plea-
surable experience of sweetness. In fact, writers
have been almost loquacious on the subject. In
The Paradise or Garden of the Fathers, Volume
II, page 44, one finds:

Abba Poemen used to say, "The certain sign that a
monk is a monk is made known by trials," and again,
page 47: "John Volab, who made entreaty unto God,
and [his] passions were removed from him said unto a
famous old man, 'I perceive that my soul is at rest.
. . .' Then the old man said unto him, 'Go and entreat
God to let war and strife come unto thee again, for it is
through war and strife that the soul advanceth in spiritual
excellence!' "

Cassian, the authority on the spiritual life for
all time, develops the subject through several

---

[26] *Spiritual Life and Prayer,* according to Holy Scripture and
Tradition, translated from the French by the Benedictines of
Stanbrook. Chap. xiv, pp. 213-218.

chapters. The ninth book of his *Institutes* is
devoted to the subject of Dejection, and in the
opening chapter he writes:

> In our fifth combat we have to resist the pangs of
> gnawing dejection: for if this, through separate attacks
> made at random, has secured an opportunity of gaining
> possession of our mind, it keeps us back at all times from
> all insight in divine contemplation, and utterly ruins and
> depresses the mind that has fallen away from its complete
> state of purity. It does not allow it to say its prayers
> with its usual gladness of heart, nor permit it to rely on
> the comfort of reading the sacred writings, nor suffer it
> to be quiet and gentle with the brethren; it makes it im-
> patient and rough in all the duties of work and devotion.

To give the proper emphasis to quotations from
Cassian it may be well to interject that an immense
number of manuscripts of his *Institutes* and *Con-
ferences,* written in the late fourth or early fifth
century, still remain scattered throughout the li-
braries of Europe; this in itself is evidence of the
high estimation in which they were held throughout the Middle Ages and the authority they possessed as expositions of the religious life. Moreover, Cassiodorus recommends them highly, as
does St. Benedict, who enjoined that the *Confer-
ences* should be read daily by the monks of his
Order.[27]

---

[27] Prolegomena to *op. cit.* p. 186; also *Catholic Encyclopedia,*
Vol. III, p. 404.

Of the value of this spiritual malady and the purpose for which it should serve, Cassian says in Chapter ix of the same book:

And so we must see that dejection is only useful to us in one case, when we yield to it either in penance for sin, or through being influenced with the desire of perfection, or the contemplation of future blessedness.

With all of this the *Ancren Riwle* is in complete accord:

In like manner, our Lord sometimes leaveth us alone, and withdraweth His grace, His comfort, and His support, so that we may feel no delight in any good that we do, nor any satisfaction of heart; and yet, at that very time our dear Father loveth us never the less, but doth it for the great love that He hath for us . . . and therefore, upon some occasion, He leaveth thee alone, that thou mayest understand thine own feebleness, and call for His aid, and cry aloud for Him.[28]

Blessed Juliana, whose penetration and insight into things spiritual are receiving wide recognition to-day, has much the same to say:

And all this brought our Lord suddenly to my mind, and shewed these words and said: I am ground of thy beseeching: first it is my will that thou have it; and after, I make thee to will it; and after I make to beseech it. . . . Pray inwardly, though thou thinketh it

---

[28] *Ancren Riwle,* pp. 230-232.

savour thee not: for it is profitable, though thou feel
not, though thou see nought; yea, though thou think
thou canst not.   For in dryness and in barrenness, in
sickness and in feebleness, then is thy prayer well-
pleasant to me though thou thinketh it savour thee nought
but little.[29]

In Chapter xi, the Two Ways of Christian Life
(Active and Contemplative) of the *English
Prose Treatises of Richard Rolle de Hampole* [30]
one finds:

If deuocyon and savour cum with-alle, kepe it and
folowe it for a tyme:—Also if deuocyon cum noghte
with mynde of the passion, stryue noghte to prese to
mekill thare-after. . . . A soule sulde mowe fele grete
comforthe if a man had grace of our Lorde, withowtten
whilke grace a mans thoghte es halfe blynde, with-owtten
savour of gastely swetnes.

His advice is precisely that of Cassian:

Also for to thynke of the wrechidnes, the myscheves
and the perills, bodily and gastely, that fallis in this lyfe,
and after that, for to thynke of the Joyes of Heuen, how
mekill blysse thare es, and how mekill Joye. . . . Noghte
for-thi me thynke it es gude on-to the that when thou
dispose the for to thynke of Godd as I hafe be-fore
saide, or one other wyse, if thi herte be dulle and myrke,

---

[29] *Revelations,* pp. 85-86.
[30] Edited from R. Thornton's Ms. by G. G. Perry, London,
1866-1921.

and felis nother witt ne savour, ne devocyon for to thynke, bot anely a naked desyre & a wayke wille.

One recognizes the source of Juliana's advice in the teachings of this spiritual director.

Probably the most popular and widely read of mediæval spiritual writers was St. Bonaventure. In view of the fact that he was named Archbishop of York by Pope Clement IV in 1265 one can well believe that his works were familiar to English scholars. *The Mirrour of the Blessed Lyf of Jesu Christ* generally attributed to him and translated by Nicholas Love, Prior of the Carthusian Monastery of Mount Grace before 1410, contains a number of very characteristic and beautiful considerations on spiritual desolation. The meditation on "How the child Jesu lafte allone in Jerusalem," makes this application:

And also here mowe we lerne, wha tyme tribulacion and angwische fallen to us, not to be hewy or moche distourbeled therby, sithe God spared not his owne moder as in that party. For he suffreth generally tribulacion to falle to hem that ben his chosen: and so they beeth tokines of his love, and to us it is expedient to have hem for many skilles (p. 75). In the forseide proces we mowe note and lerne . . . that he that ledeth goostly lyf wonder not moche, ne be not discomforted ouere heuely, thou he be som tyme so drie in soule, and so voyde of deuocioun as he were forsake of God. Where-

fore be he not in despeire there by, bot besilich seche Jesu
in holy meditaciouns and gode werkes, and specially in
deuoute prayeres, and he shal fynde hym at the laste
in dewe tyme (pp. 77, 78).

St. Bonaventure uses the example of the tem-
pest on the sea of Galilee to illustrate the
same trouble of soul. He says:

Wherefore have we no wonder though oure lord Jesu
suffered his disciples, the which he loved so specially, to
be turbled with tempests, as it is seide, and suffre tribu-
lacions: for he knew her gastely profite thereby. . . .
And no more schulle we what tribulacion so evere come
to vs gif we suffre paciently and triste fully in the helpe
of oure lord Jesu, that wole not faille vs at oure nede
(pp. 142, 143).

The great classic of the spiritual life is, of
course, the *Imitation of Christ,* attributed to
Thomas à Kempis and issued anonymously in
1418. It was translated into English as early as
1441 and was probably known in England in the
Latin some years earlier; the identity of its spirit
with that of the *Pearl* poet Professor Schofield
has pointed out. The entire third book of the
volume is devoted to "Interior Consolation"
which obviously supposes "interior desolation"
and prescribes abundantly against it.

The patience of paper rather than dearth of

material puts a limit on quotation to prove the
reality of the state of spiritual dryness and its
familiarity to masters of the spiritual life at all
periods before and during the time of the writing of *Pearl*.

While a person is in this state he thinks very
much on the ways of God in dealing variously
with different souls. Such devout meditations
have appeared in the numerous citations. He
compares his own condition with that of others
as he sees it; he thinks of the reward that is
often given to persons after only a short life, of
the heaven of baptized infants, won without a
conscious effort. He is torn between hope and
despair, between love and desperation. He realizes with equal keenness the depths of his own
unworthiness and the heights of his celestial desires. Altogether he is thoroughly uncomfortable.
Through it all he clings to the resolution that
though God slay him, yet will he trust in Him.
Experience in this condition is quite the same
as in the days of Job; probably no one understands quite so well as a religious the anguish of
spirit that was upon the man of Hus.

The ordinary antidotes which spiritual directors
have prescribed at all times against this visita-
tion are: trust in God and His grace, prayer, the
thought of heaven, absolute patience and resigna-

tion.   One finds such recommendations in the *Institutes* of Cassian, Chapter xii:

We should then be able to expel this most injurious passion (dejection) from our hearts, so that by spiritual meditation we may keep our mind constantly occupied with hope of the future and contemplation of the promised blessedness.   For in this way we shall be able to get the better of all those sorts of dejection . . . if ever with an insight into things eternal and future, and continuing immovable, we are not depressed by present accidents.

Juliana counsels resignation with her own quaint sweetness:

And also He will that we take our abidings and diseases as lightly as we may take them, and set them at naught: for the lightlier that we take them, and the less price that we set at them for love, less pain shall we have in feeling of them, and the more thank and meed shall we have for them (p. 18).

Thomas à Kempis says in the *Imitation of Christ*, Book II, Chapter viii:[31]

Thou must be naked, and carry a pure heart to God, if thou wilt attend at leisure, and see how sweet is the Lord. . . .
For when the grace of God comes to a man, then he is strong and powerful for all things; and when it de-

---

[31] The translation of the Right Reverend Richard Challoner is used for quotations.

parts, then he is poor and weak, left as it were only to stripes.

In these he must not be dejected nor despair; but stand with an even mind, resigned to the will of God and bear, for the glory of Jesus Christ, whatever shall befall him; because after winter comes summer; after night the day returns; after a storm there follows a great calm.

Here is the absolute pattern of humble resignation and abandonment, the fruit of desolation, and the ideal realized with beautiful perfection in the last pages of the poem, *Pearl*.

This stripping from one all vesture of self, this utter nakedness of soul which leaves no single barrier between it and God, is the ultimate and perfect fruit of spiritual dejection. Of course, no one presumes to achieve it at all without God's grace or gift, nor perfectly until one reaches heaven. But the desire for it is the great impelling force of all ardent, and particularly of all mystical souls. As Juliana of Norwich inimitably says: "It is not God's will that we follow the feeling of pains in sorrow and mourning for them, but suddenly pass over, and hold us in the endless liking that is in God." And "I wist well that He that bound me so sore, He should unbind me when He would. . . . Mightily, wisely and wilfully I chose Jesu to be my Heaven" (pp. 42-45).

CHAPTER III

SPIRITUAL BACKGROUNDS AND SETTING

So moving and direct is the sweep of Chaucerian narrative in the fourteenth century that one, watching its splendid and resistless flow, forgets that undercurrents are at work, dominating its course, cutting all its bed but the very shore line, swaying the entire stream in directions which the subtle surface scarce betrays. It looks a stream almost entirely worldly, almost entirely secular, and in its sources pagan quite as much as Christian. It gives no hint of tides of sanctity, of currents of mysticism beneath. As a matter of fact, more than a good part of all the writing of the century was religious in its traditions, subject-matter, and purpose. The drama was almost entirely so; prose divided itself between secular and religious interests, chronicles, translations and paraphrases of the Bible, catechisms, sermons, treatises, and proverbs; narrative poetry was as devoted to saints' legends and Mary stories as to romances and fabliaux; and the secular lyric was inconspicuous beside the religious lyric of the period. Nineteenth century evaluations have sometimes lost sight of these facts and proportions.

Readily as the *Pearl* lends itself to a purely spiritual interpretation, this interpretation, if a single peculiarly personal reading of a solitary poem, unfortified and unaccompanied by a representative number of similar works demanding similar treatment, would obviously fall through. If, however, it can be ranged with a whole body of contemporaneous religious writing, quintessentially mystical in insight and intensity and poetic in expression, its case is quite secure.

Straight through the twelfth, thirteenth, and fourteenth centuries one feels the steady pulse of an intense spirituality in Europe. It indicates a rich and active *interior life,* a consciousness of God, a preoccupation with sanctity. It expressed itself in specific lives of sanctity, and in a body of writings biographical of such lives. Records, Acts, Revelations, Dialogues, Autobiographies of persons conspicuous for virtue were multiplied; I shall mention only the most conspicuous. The theme is consistently the union of God with man and of man with God; this union is accomplished frequently through the mystical experience of ecstasy; it is accompanied by temptations, darknesses and aridities; it culminates in the vision and possession of God. As background, as foreground, as setting and stage furniture it fits perfectly the demands of the *Pearl*.

Mysticism in fourteenth century England was an established and well organized manner of religious life, as rich in ancestry as it has been in its posterity. It rested on the most authentic of traditions; the traditions of St. Bonaventure and St. Bernard, of St. Francis of Assisi and Blessed Angela of Foligno, of Duns Scotus and Dionysius, and ultimately on Plotinus and St. John. It had become articulate earlier, in the *Ancren Riwle;* it found abundant companionship in German schools of Master Eckhart and his successors, Suso and Tauler; and in the Flemish school of Ruysbroeck from which came Thomas à Kempis and Master Peterson. It was part of the rich flowering of the great mystical movement of the twelfth century. The leaders of this movement were Bernard of Clairvaux and Hugh of St. Victor.

In an enterprise with perfection and divinity for its objective, it is foolish and crass to assign preëminence to its captains, or to say who was greatest among men whose ambition it was to be least. It was these two, however, who gave direction, method, and stability to a religious mode, the very sensitivity of which might otherwise have

deteriorated into fanaticism. Bernard of Clairvaux, born at Dijon in 1090, was just six years
older than Hugh of St. Victor and lived twelve
years longer. He was blessed abbot of Clairvaux by William of Champeaux, the founder of
the cloister of St. Victor and the spiritual father
of Hugh. So the lives of the three were knit
in a bond that was life-long. It is as pretty as
the story of Chaucer and Gower and Strode.
Hugh, being the philosopher preëminently, formu-
lated a code of the soul's progress to union with
God. Knowledge he considered not an end in
itself but a means to the mystical life, the life
of spiritual as opposed to physical experience and
knowledge. Thought, meditation, and contemplation he regarded respectively as the natural, the
supernatural, and the intuitive avenues of intercourse with God, the three eyes of the rational
soul. [32] There is a challenge and a charm in the
neatness and perspicuity of his theory. And it is
significant that thousands in his day and later
have been able to reduce it to practice.

---

[32] J. B. Haureau, *Hugues de St. Victor et l'edition de ses
œuvres*, Paris, 1859.

J. B. Haureau, *Les œuvres de Hugues de Saint Victor; essai
critique*, Paris, 1886. The chief mystical doctrines of Hugh of
St. Victor are found in his works under the titles of "De
Vanitate Mundi," and "Contemplatione et eius speciebus."

De Wulf, *Histoire de la philosophie médiévale*, Louvain,
1905, pp. 212-215, 228-230.

Bernard of Clairvaux should have been born in the twentieth century. He grew up with a positive ambition to excel in literature, to get into print! He spent years in studying and writing poetry, and other years in a Crusade involving fierce, selfish kings and keen-minded, wayward princesses. He wrote a rule for the Knights Templars; he wrote love songs to the Blessed Virgin, the Lady of his delight.[33] He was a very genius for initiative, versatility, address. Yet, if he were to be described in a single word, that one word would be "mystic." Love was for him the fulfilling of the law. The manner of loving God, he says in *De Amore Dei*, is to love Him without measure; then with the unfailing but unexpected method of the true mystic, he enumerates and describes the different degrees of this love. His earlier work, *De Gradibus Superbiæ et Humilitatis*, sets a pattern for spiritual writing as easy to trace as any of the story or romance devices, the dream or the pilgrimage, for instance. His devotion to the Blessed Virgin he expressed in numberless exquisite hymns and

---

[33] *Works of St. Bernard*, translated by Eales and Hodges, London, 1889, containing "De Gradibus Superbiæ," "Homilies— De Laudibus Mariæ." "De Laudibus Novae Militiae," "De Amore Dei," 530 Letters, Sermons, etc.

Hefele, *Concilien Geschichte*, Freiburg, 1886, Vol. V, p. 402.
Alletz, *Dictionnaire Portatif des Conciles*, Paris, 1758, p. 537.

prayers, notably the *Memorare* which was and is even to-day, next to the *Hail Mary,* the most common petition to our Lady. He wrote a series of homilies, *De Laudibus Mariæ.* His praise of Mary through the written word is a part of mediæval literary method; it enters into all religious writing, and takes on a devotional manner in works of a personal nature. It is thus that one meets it in *Pearl*—stanzas xxxvi-xxxviii. Bossuet says of St. Bernard that "piety was his all"; it must have been a very winning piety for the saint himself was an irresistible person. Men loved him, his ways, his words, even his sermons, and when they could no longer listen to them, they read them. So it is that in fourteen hundred and before, we find scribes in any number of English monasteries translating and paraphrasing the mystical works of Bernard of Clairvaux.[34]

Ignoring for the moment the fire of Franciscan spirituality that ran through thirteenth century Europe, and particularly that fine flame kindled by it, Angela of Foligno, setting aside also the

---

[34] M. G. Segar, *Mediæval Anthology*, New York, 1915, "A Song of Love-Longing," p. 14; "Stabat Mater," p. 55; "St. Bernard," from "Man's Foes," p. 102.

R. Rolle, *Form of Perfect Living* and Other Prose Treatises, rendered into Modern English by G. E. Hodgson, London, 1910, pp. 6, 121, 125, 131, 138.

W. Hilton, *Scale of Perfection,* London, 1870, p. 41.

Revelations of St. Gertrude which shone beside
these, I take that seraphic doctor, lecturer, professor of the University of Paris, Cardinal of
Albano, St. Bonaventure as a central figure in
the centuries and movements under consideration.
Living between 1221 and 1274, he was as important a figure at the seats of learning and the
courts of Italy, Spain, France, and Germany as
he was at the chapters of his Order or the coun-
cils of the Church.   In himself he combined the
profound learning and the beautiful piety which
are the finest fruits of the Middle Ages.   As a
mystic he developed and continued the Victorine
theories and in his *De Triplici Via,* sometimes
wrongly called *Incendium Amoris,* he presents a
summary of the perfected doctrines laid down
by Hugh of St. Victor.   His *Vita Mystica* was
for a long time attributed to St. Bernard, which
makes his relation to twelfth century spirituality
close enough.   Now to make the transition to
England.   His pupil at Paris, John Peckham, was
later made Archbishop of Canterbury, and is now
considered to be the author of a rhythmical mystical treatise, *Philomela,* for a time supposed to
have been written by Bonaventure.   He himself
was named Archbishop of York by Pope Clement
IV in 1265 but refused to accept the honor.   So,
though he never visited England in any capacity,

his works are more frequently translated and paraphrased than those of any other man by writers during the next century. And the fifteenth century saw fifty editions of his books. Which is sufficiently indicative of his influence.[35]

Of the place of his father in God, Francis of Assisi, in the general setting of mediæval spirituality, it is hardly necessary to speak. The miracles of his life and love have enjoyed continued and, at present, accelerated exploitation. One can fit Brothers Giles and Juniper quite readily into the general scheme, also. But there is another character, fugitive and ordinary and completely significant. It is Angela of Foligno. This woman, so far as biography informs us, was a commonplace, frivolous, sinful woman when she came under the influence of the sons of St. Francis of Assisi. Hers is a parallel to the conversion of Magdalen. She died on January 8, 1309, leaving in a small diary the record of her spiritual reformation.[36] In it she says:

"In my progress toward the road of penance I

---

[35] Doctoris Seraphicae S. Bonaventurae S. R. E. Episcopis Cardinalis *Opera Omnia, Quaracchi*, 1882-1902. Volume VIII contains Bonaventure's mystical writing, his exposition of the interior life. Giovanni di Fidanzi Bonaventura, *Opera Omnia*, Paris, 1864. Volumes VIII and XII contain his mystical writings.

[36] Accessible in Algar Thorold's *Catholic Mysticism*, London, 1900, p. 90.

traveled by eighteen spiritual steps, before I knew the imperfection of my life." These she enumerates as: knowledge of sin, shame, penance, consideration of the mercy of God, self-knowledge, sight of the cross, knowledge of the cause of Christ's death, knowledge of the way of the cross, apparition of Christ crucified, flight from the world, memory of the passion, vision of the heart of Christ, clearer knowledge of Him, experience of the passion, infused knowledge of the Pater Noster, increased faith through the Blessed Virgin, delight in prayer. The character of her revelations is particularly pertinent. She tells of fearful temptations, the nightmares of past vices, of darkness and pride and physical infirmity. Then comes the sweetness and light of vision and a voice saying: [37]

I am the Holy Spirit, who come to thee to give thee consolation such as thou hast never before tasted. . . . My beloved, My spouse, love Me, all that thou doest pleases Me . . . when thou eatest, when thou drinkest, when thou sleepest . . . thy whole life pleases Me completely, if thou lovest Me.

Of her own attitude toward these visions she says:

I was certain, beyond any doubt, that He Who had spoken to me was God, and because of His sweetness and

[37] *Op. cit.*, p. 123.

my grief, I wept, wishing to die. . . . And I had a very great desire to die and leave the world, so that I might not lose that sweetness and delight.

A desire which the *Pearl* poet paraphrases, "Delight as draws me, eye and ear;—I would be there" (ll. 1153-1155) and all mystics share. Her language and attitude are unmistakable but not quite isolated, one thinks, remembering that Dante was wrapt in his three-fold vision at this very hour. Another revelation illustrates two things: the mystic's unfailing devotion to the mother of God, and the soul's ability to contemplate its own self and its activities. This is a possibility of prime importance in the *Pearl*. She says:

Once, in Lent, it seemed to me that I was very dry and without devotion. And I prayed God . . . and then the eyes of my soul were opened and I saw Love coming toward me [the opening situation in *Pearl*]. . . . And I know not any similitude for Its colour. . . . And love came toward me, as it were, like a scythe. This similitude is not to be taken as regards measurable quantity, but Love was like a scythe, in that It appeared and withdrew. . . . My soul spoke within me, imploring Love not to make her languish through so great love, for I reckoned life to be death. And she invoked first the Blessed Virgin and then the Apostles. . . . And I saw in myself two divisions . . . and in one division I saw love and every good which was God's and not mine, [this may be comparable to the poet's vision] and in the other I saw myself, dry, and I saw I had nothing of good belonging to me [a clear picture of the poet's desolate self].

Such abjection is a consummation devoutly to be wished by the true mystic and the infallible test which distinguishes him from the false one. That the mystic is not a mere automaton or praying-machine one feels in this lively give and take with the Deity:

And He said to me, "I have an immense love for thee, but I do not show Myself to thee, yea rather do I hide Myself from thee." And my soul said to Him, "Wherefore dost Thou love me so?" . . . "Verily," He replied to me, "so great is the love that I have reposed in thee, that I scarcely remember thy defects, although Mine eyes see them." . . . And my soul felt . . . and saw that the Eyes of God were looking at her, into which Eyes she looked, and had therein so great delight that no man could describe it. . . . And therewith He told me that He had concealed much love from me because I could not bear it. And my soul replied, "If Thou art God Almighty, Thou canst make me able to bear it." And He replied, "If I were to do so, thou wouldst no longer hunger for Me. Therefore will I not do so, for, whilest Thou art in this life, it is My will that thou shouldst hunger for Me, and desire Me, and languish for Me." [38]

---

[38] *Op. cit.*, p. 143.

Two other women in the history of mysticism might well have perpetrated such a piece of heavenly impertinence, Juliana of Norwich and Teresa of Avila. It is beautiful to watch the centuries retreat before the intimacy of such a spirit. The "madding" of the *Pearl* poet would certainly have pushed him to some such excess; I like to think that his masculine restraint as much as virtuous resignation held him back. At all events, Angela of Foligno in her exposition of her conversion, with its periods of dryness, of consoling love, of encouragement through consideration of the passion of Christ and devotion to Mary, is a precursor of the *Pearl* poet.

Completely contemporary with Angela of Foligno and thoroughly united with her in the pursuit of the Franciscan ideal, Ramon Lull excelled her in the headlong activity of his enterprises for heavenly Love and the burning ardor of the records he has left us. A more romantic knight God never had. Literally shocked into decency himself, he had scarcely realized his own conversion before he set out to convert Jews, Mohammedans, infidels in general. His zeal was that of a lover; love was the passion of his life and Christ was its Object. Being a native of Majorca, he wrote in the idiom of Catalonia, and his *Blanquerna* constitutes an essential document

in Spanish mysticism.   One section of it, entitled
the *Book of the Lover and the Beloved*,[39] presents the most striking of parallels with *Pearl*.
The comparison is worked out with some care and
detail in Chapter iv, which obviates further discussion of the book and the writer in this place.

This quest for spiritual relatives presents all
the fascination of a search for some long-lost
cousins with about equal chances of embarrass-
ments.   These last are happily absent here.   Between the years of 1256 and 1301 (1302?) there
lived in the vicinity of Eisleben a Benedictine
nun, Gertrude, whom posterity has seen fit to call
"the Great."   She represents no sudden spiritual
ascent from sin to conversion, but rather the
steady progress in degree from innocence to
sanctity.   Entering the Benedictine convent at the
age of five, she became, before twenty, a profound
and brilliant scholar.   Her entrance into the religious life was a consecration of her splendid
achievements.   It meant a continuance of work
with a difference of intention.   Her life was that
of the ordinary Benedictine nun, of whom she is
regarded as the perfect type.   When she was
twenty-six years old: "On Monday before the

---

[39] R. Lull, *Book of the Lover and the Beloved,* translated
from the Catalan with an introductory essay by E. Allison
Peers, New York, 1923.

Feast of the Purification . . . after Compline"—
so explicit is she—God manifested Himself to her
in the first of His revelations. Her account of it
is disconcerting in prosaic detail:

> Being, then, in the middle of our dormitory, at the
> hour I have named, and having inclined to an ancient re-
> ligious, according to our rule, on raising my head I beheld
> Thee, my most loving Love, and my Redeemer, surpassing
> in beauty the children of men, under the form of a youth
> of sixteen years, beautiful and amiable, and attracting
> my heart and my eyes by the infinite light of Thy glory
> . . . and standing before me, Thou didst utter these
> words, full of tenderness and sweetness: "Thy salvation
> is at hand . . . I will receive you, and inebriate you
> with the torrent of My celestial delights." [40]

Her *Revelations* (*Insinuationes Divinæ Pietatis*)
—St. Gertrude wrote entirely in Latin—continue
with matter-of-fact precision as to hour and
place, to record her reception of the stigmata
of Christ, the wound of divine Love, the sweet
Divinity of Christ under the form of His infancy. Her manner is as unimaginative as a cook-
book and yet the thing she has to record is In-
effability Itself. It is no wonder that Blosius
and Suarez and Francis de Sales received their
spiritual direction from her. She herself ad-
hered closely to Benedictine traditions and

---

[40] *The Life and Revelations of St. Gertrude,* London, p. 72.

98668

methods, but apart from them, sought Bernard of Clairvaux for her guide. And in that she identified herself with the Christian Europe of her day.

This is the briefest possible indication of the thirteenth century European background for fourteenth century English spiritual autobiography. The age held a Boccaccio and a Petrarch and a Dante for Chaucer; it held a Bernard and a Bonaventure and a Dante for the mystics. It is more than rich in material, perfectly consistent in its traditions, and universally autobiographical in expression. The quotations here given have been cited from prose works. But it must not be forgotten that this is the age of the great Latin hymns of the Church, most of them anonymous; the *Stabat Mater*, which has a whole multitude of Middle English variations, the *Jesu Dulcis Memoria*, the *Ave Maris Stella*, the *Pange Lingua* and *Bone Pastor* of St. Thomas Aquinas, to mention only those that reappear most frequently in English religious lyrics and which record intense spiritual relations between the soul and God. There was the whole body of Bernardine and Franciscan and Dominican poetry; above all, there were the *Convito* and the *Divine Comedy* of Dante.

This mediæval mystical impulse was not circumscribed; no more was it sporadic. It fed and was fed by such blazing brands as St. Dominic, Albert the Great, St. Thomas Aquinas. Other sons of St. Dominic identified themselves with it more completely. John Eckhart was the foremost of these. He was born near Gotha in 1260. He entered the Order of Preachers and taught philosophy successively at Paris, Strasburg, and Cologne. He was a distinguished orator and a master of German prose; he was preëminently a mystic. His philosophy was based on Albertus Magnus, his theology on Aquinas, and though he quotes frequently from John Scotus and the Pseudo-Areopagite, his mysticism is that of Hugh of St. Victor. Our history concatenates as well as even Anatole France might desire. Here is the perfect link. Meister Eckhart, as he was called, met in Cologne Henry Suso and John Tauler, two of the most significant mystics of their own or any age. He was their teacher, their inspirer, and the bond of closest friendship between them. Of his works only prologues and fragments remain, dealing for the most part with the essence of God and the relations between God and man.

Suso, the elder of his two aptest pupils, was born in Constance in 1295 and died in Ulm in 1366. His life, in intent, is a parallel to Dante's.

In his eighteenth year he abandoned the careless, worldly habits of his youth and gave himself up to be the servant of Divine Wisdom. The fruit of this service and the visions and ecstasies with which it was visited one finds in his *Little Book of Truth (Buchlein der Wahrheit)*, called the most difficult of the writings of the German mystics. His *Little Book of Eternal Wisdom* represents the reverse of this obscurity and belongs, in its simplicity of style and universal appeal, with the *Homilies* of St. Bernard and the *Following of Christ*. Enlarged into what Suso called the *Horologium Sapientiæ,* it became the favorite book of spiritual reading at the close of the Middle Ages in Germany, the Netherlands, France, Italy, and England. The mutual love of God and man was the preoccupation of his life and the theme of all his writing.[41]

Suso's dear friend, John Tauler, was born at the opening of the century which closed with Chaucer's death. He died in 1361. Tauler joined the Order of St. Dominic and led a life of asceticism and study. The *Meisterbuch* has, until quite recently, been regarded as a partial record of it, but this with a body of treatises and hymns formerly attributed to him, are now re-

---

[41] *The Life of Blessed Henry Suso,* by himself, translated from the original German by T. F. Knox, London.

garded as spurious. Out of the sermons duly authenticated shines the central doctrine of his mysticism, the blessed contemplation and knowledge of the divine Nature of God. He takes his doctrine from St. Thomas Aquinas but is perhaps more ardent and fiery-hearted in the pursuit of it.

Born seven years before Tauler and surviving him by a decade, John Ruysbroeck is regarded as undoubtedly the foremost of Flemish mystics. He lived for a long time a life of extreme austerity and retirement, from which he emerged in about 1343 to refute by word and writing various heretical sects of the day, notably the Brethren of the Free Spirit. His company, advice, and direction were sought by men of all places and conditions; there is mention of a visit from Tauler. His writings were multiplied in the Netherlands and Germany and made their way to England early in the fifteenth century. Gerard Groot loved him as a friend and venerated him as a spiritual father; together they formed the community of Windesheim which in a quarter of a century was to father Thomas à Kempis. Quite naturally his life of out-of-door meditations, wanderings, and musings blossomed into the most exquisite of ascetic works, notably *The Spiritual Espousals* and *Love's Gradatory*. The former Maeterlinck has put into French. It is divided into three books, treating respectively of the active, the interior, and the contemplative life and is written on an almost esoteric plane of mysticism, the theme of each book being "Behold, the Bridegroom cometh; prepare the way for Him." The various paths of grace by which the Bridegroom comes to the soul, His bride, the various paths of virtue by which the soul hastens to her Beloved, their meeting and embrace are themes which only the initiated can follow with reverence and understanding. *Love's Gradatory* is the third of a series of treatises apparently addressed to Margaret of Meerbeke, Superior in the convent of Poor Clares, Brussels, and repeats the figure of a ladder which one meets constantly in mystical writing and which could be pushed back for its source to the dream of Jacob. One finds it in the *Acts of Sts. Perpetua and Felicitas,* second century, and in the *Rule of St. Benedict.* St. John Climacus entitles one of his books *The Ladder of Holiness.* The idea probably came to the blessed John from the Seraphic Doctor, Bonaventure. The steps in *Love's Gradatory* to God are good will, poverty, chastity, humility, from which spring rivers of obedience, meekness, patience, and abandonment. The figure and the virtues are equally familar to lovers of

the *Pearl*. (Stanzas ix, xxix, xxx, xxxi.)   His
fifth step is nobility of virtue, the sixth, clear
intuition, and the seventh, complete union with
God.[42]

Born under the same star of fourteenth century mysticism as Ruysbroeck, Thomas à Kempis
embraced the counsels of perfection in the Order
of Canons Regular at Mount St. Agnes, Windesheim, in 1399. Out of his years of rich and
active spirituality spent there, came the *Imitation
of Christ,* a classic on mysticism, a little epic of
the inner life.[43]   It is one of the most generally
known and widely read of spiritual autobiographies, and, which is more pertinent here, a close
parallel to *Pearl*. It consists of four books, the
first treating of the spiritual life in general, the
second of interior things, the third of interior
consolation, and the fourth of the Blessed Sacrament. The arrangement of the books in this
order, though followed in most editions, is arbitrary. That, however, is beside the point; it is à
Kempis's study of interior consolation that con-

---

[42] John Ruysbroeck, *Love's Gradatory,* translated by Mother
St. Jerome, New York, 1914.

[43] On the question of the authorship of the *Imitation,* see
"Who was the Author of 'The Imitation of Christ'?" by Sir
F. R. Cruise, M.D., *Catholic Truth Society*, London, 1898;
also *Deductio Critica* by Eusebii Amort, Wolher, 1761; also
The Life of the Venerable Thomas à Kempis by Dom Vincent
Scully, C. R. L., New York, 1901.

cerns the student of *Pearl*. The book is written in dialogue form for the most part, the
speakers being Christ and the Disciple. In this
it is like the poem. The last ten chapters of
the book are devoted to a consideration of interior
desolation, of the necessity of complete resignation to God, of the grace of God and the different motions of nature and grace, of consideration of the passion, of not searching into the secret
judgments of God, and of fixing one's confidence
entirely on God.[44] The *Pearl* follows precisely
these lines. There is the poet's desolation, stanzas i-v; then the vision of the Maiden who, in
stanzas xxvi, xxvii, xxix, xxx prescribes conformity
to God's will; there follows in stanzas xlii-lvi an
exposition, illustrated by the parable of the laborers, of the grace of God; a brief consideration
of the passion and death of Christ in stanzas lxvii
and lxviii, and in the last five stanzas the poet's
entire surrender to the Divine Will. The parallelism thus briefly indicated is substantiated with
quotations in Chapter iv. Here, it adds the *Imitation* to the conspicuous spiritual autobiographies
of which I hold the *Pearl* to be a shining and
beautiful example.

---

[44] Thomas à Kempis, *Imitation of Christ,* translated from the
Latin by the Rt. Reverend Challoner, D.D., New York.

One other name will make this group representative although a hundred would not make it complete. It is St. Catherine of Siena, who was born in 1347 and died at the age of thirty-three, a significant and mystical span. She was a master of her own most bitter and evil age who, while accomplishing the return of the pope to Rome and a multitude of lesser spiritual and diplomatic victories, led a life of ecstasy, experienced her well-known espousals with Christ, and left as a contribution to mystical literature a voluminous correspondence and her *Dialogues,* dictated to her secretaries while in ecstasy, a book of "ecclesiastical mysticism," a classic of the age and land of Petrarch and Boccaccio. Her treatise on Divine Providence in the *Dialogues* begins:

The soul, who is lifted by a very great and yearning desire for the honor of God and the salvation of souls, begins by exercising herself . . . in the ordinary virtues, remaining in the cell of self-knowledge. . . . But, in no way, does the creature receive such a taste of the truth, or so brilliant a light therefrom, as by means of humble and continuous prayer, founded on knowledge of herself and of God [or as the maiden in *Pearl* says to the poet]:

Stint from thy strife and cease to chide,
And seek His grace full swift and sure;
Thy prayer may His pity touch,
And Mercy may show forth her craft. (ll. 353-357)

Prayer thus, by desire and affection, and union of love, makes her another Himself; for, she explains:

> God was not wont to conceal, from the eye of her intellect, the love which He had for His servants, but rather . . . to say: "Open the eye of thy intellect and gaze into Me. . . . And look at those creatures who, among the beauties which I have given to the soul, creating her in My image and similitude, are clothed with the nuptial garment; that is, united with Me through love." [45]

or as one finds it in *Pearl*:

> Wherefore each soul that hath no taint
> is to that Lamb a wife ador'd. (ll. 845-846)

and again,

> It gladd'neth the Lamb; our care is cast;
> He maketh mirth at every meal;
> of each the bliss is bravest and best,
> and no one's honor is yet the less. (ll. 860-864)

One might quote to much greater length; these passages seem particularly pertinent as paralleling themes and figures in the *Pearl*. The two books must have been written at almost precisely the same time. The language as well as the

---

[45] *The Dialogues of St. Catherine of Siena*, translated from the original Italian by Algar Thorold, London, 1907, pp. 26-27.

experiences of St. Catherine are familiar to all
mystics in varying degrees; hers is almost the
widest compass of all, ranging from extreme common sense to consummate union with God.   Her
counsels on contrition and the practice of virtue
are uncompromising; "a man proves his patience
on his neighbors," she says, "when he receives
injuries from them."   One guesses the spiritual
heights from which she regards even sin from
this line:

Whether man will or no, he cannot help making an act
of love. . . . Wherefore, I show you that in My house
are many mansions, and that I wish for no other thing
than love. . . .

the theme, the refrain to the mystic's changeless
litany.

In an essay on "The Spiritual Life in Mediæval
England" introductory to his edition of Walter
Hilton's *Scale of Perfection*,[46] the Reverend J. B.
Dalgairns says:

We know that the time was marked by an outburst
of mystical life in Germany, and that Eckhart, Tauler,
and Blessed Henry Suso are proofs of the existence of
a deeply speculative as well as religious spirit, but we
are not prepared to find it in England.

---

[46] W. Hilton, *The Scale of Perfection,* London, 1870. Introduction, XV.

And yet conditions in England were not entirely unfavorable to mysticism. A little too philosophic, perhaps; a little too scientific even; and quite too politically and ecclesiastically involved to provide the most desirable opportunities for detachment and other-worldliness. Yet there were possibilities; there were impulses; there were seeds which flowered with the school of Richard Rolle. John of Salisbury,[47] one of the most cultured scholars of his day, was a personal friend of Bernard of Clairvaux; Bishop Grosseteste in the next century touched mysticism at another point in providing for English translations of the writings of Dionysius, the Psuedo-Areopagite.[48] But the background of English mysticism is a profound and indigenous element of English life itself. Some scholars have found in the brooding awe for natural phenomena, the supersensitiveness to an all-encompassing power so characteristic of Old English poetry an inherent or natural mysticism. Mystical meanings have been read into *Beowulf* and read out of the works of Cynewulf. *Christ* unquestionably speaks the language of vision, of almost familiar intimacy with

---

[47] Schaarschmidt, *Joannes Saresberiensis nach Leben und Studien, Schriften und Philosophie,* Leipsic, 1862.

[48] Stevenson, *Robert Grosseteste, Bishop of Lincoln,* London, 1899.

the Divine. The *Phœnix* is another bit of deific biography; the *Dream of the Rood* makes the holy Cross itself tell its own mystical story. These are not merely pious paraphrases of Scripture nor religious treatises. They are expressions of a very clear, very definite, and a supernatural understanding of Christ. They imply a nativeness to God, an intuitive knowledge of Him and express the greatest tenderness of personal love for Him. Mysticism is precisely this. And representative early English literature, indicated here, is saturated with it.[49]

Thirteenth century England supplied a complete text book on the interior life in the form of the *Ancren Riwle* to which reference has already been made. And in Alexander of Hales, the Franciscan philosopher, it possessed an influence entirely comparable to St. Bonaventure on the continent. Their theological doctrines are identical.[50] And for poetry of love-longing, for allegories of precious gems it offers the exquisite *Luve Ron*[51] attributed to the Franciscan Friar Thomas of Hales and comparable in many details

---

[49] *English Mystics,* by G. E. Hodgson (Milwaukee, 1922), has an interesting chapter on this subject.

[50] Stöckl, *Geschichte der Philosophie des Mittelalters,* Vol. II, Maintz, 1865. Turner, *History of Philosophy,* p. 326 seq., Boston, 1905.

[51] M. G. Segar, *A Mediæval Anthology,* New York, 1915, p. 49.

to *Pearl* as has already been pointed out. It has the earlier poem *On God Ureisun of Ure Lefde,*[52] written perhaps by Edmund Rich, Archbishop of Canterbury, as well as the religious poetry of William de Shoreham to which reference is made in Chapter iv. In a country which, for three centuries had been speaking the language of spiritual allegory, which plowed its fields to a mystic language of prayer, which saw in animals and trees types and figures of Christ and Redemption, which proudly dedicated the flower of its manhood and womanhood to a mystic marriage with the Lamb of God in religious life, the fourteenth century outburst of fervor in literary form is neither surprising nor unwarranted.

The stage is set, the prologue has been spoken in four languages,—enter Richard Rolle. His is the first name that emerges in England to identify this school of religious expression with those on the continent. He was born in Thornton-le-Dale, Yorkshire, about 1300. His early home education, his subsequent exchange of the academic garb, and the logic and philosophy of Oxford for an improvised hermit's habit—a strange hybrid affair, half his sister's dress, half John Dalton's cloak—and the science of Divine Love

---

[52] Konrath, *Anglia,* pp. 42-85.

were the beginnings of an other-worldly mode of life and thought which not a few of his contemporaries were quick to understand and eager to follow.   Of his return from Oxford Mary Segar says:[53]

Yorkshire at that time (1319) boasted fourteen great abbeys, sixty priories, thirty friaries, thirteen cells, and twenty collegiate churches, so that, in coming home to give himself entirely to spiritual things, Rolle was not coming to a land where his ideal would be misunderstood.

He gave himself up to a life of evangelizing, of instructing, comparable to nothing within nineteenth century experience so much as General Booth and the Salvation Army.   Up and down the country he went, from Richmondshire to Doncaster, and on to Hampole, preaching, teaching, writing, leading an exterior and interior life of intensest spirituality.   George Perry says of his tremendous activities:[54]

In foreign collections his name figures as a writer of Latin treatises under the singular disguise of Pampolitanus. . . .

[53] *Catholic World,* August, 1924, "Alexandria and the Mystical Writings of the Middle Ages," p. 642.
[54] *English Prose Treatises of Richard Rolle of Hampole,* Preface, Vol. VIII. Early English Text Society.

A cursory glance at the manuscript catalogues of our chief collections will at once reveal the fact that Richard Rolle of Hampole was one of the most prolific writers of his day, and the fact of the preservation of so large a mass of MSS., either his or attributed to him, testifies to the great estimation in which he was once held.

He was the voice of authority upon what abundant evidence proves to have been a recognized and established form of spirituality. His short treatises are as definite as military manuals or short-story text books. He speaks of the matter, the particular technique, the problems, the perfections of a life of love and union with God, without apology or preface or special plea. In reading him, or indeed any of his followers, one has no sense that the writer is feeling for an uncertain audience, that he is the voice of one crying in the wilderness. Delight in God and a sensible yearning for Him one might not suppose to have been an atmospheric condition of fourteenth century England. But here is an Oxford student—a possible university Freshman—who deliberately gives up his B.A., not for any mediæval Hollywood or New York, not for London or France or Italy, but for an anchorhold and the songs of angels. The situation is significant. The century and locality that saw a young Chaucer buried to his ears in business and Boccaccio, enjoyed the unique spectacle of a spiritual Quixote, clad in a makeshift habit of gray and white faring forth on an enterprise of more courtly Love, of more heavenly business for which his *calor, canor,* and *dulcor* were the current coins. Which means that a *Romaunt of the Rose* and a *Pearl* can exist in the same period and speak somewhat the same language and yet be as far apart as earth and heaven.

His counsels, addressed to a certain Margaret Kirby, are such counsels as one reads in the *Pearl*—the fire of devotion is a spark of divine love for God, sent by Him, and consists of an earnest longing for heavenly things which works, as he says, "Gastely comforte and gastely swetnes in a mans saul." It is, however, but the beginning of the full and perfect love of God which cannot be reached in this world, where we must "walk by faith and not by sight." He knows the zeal of the over-eager in all its unreasonable extremes; his quotation of their "A, Lorde, brynge me to Thi blysse!" anticipates the importunity of the *Pearl* poet, "Now lead me to that merry spot" (l. 936). The means of fostering the spiritual life he lays down with the directness of authority; contrition, prayer, meditation upon the different virtues, always without anxiety —"take esyle that will cum"—consideration of

the lives of the saints and "also the mynd of oure
lady Saynt Marie abowne all other sayntes. . . .
The behaldyngd of the fairehede of this bliysid
saule sulde stirre a mans herte vn-to gastely con-
forthe gretly"; and so the poet found. So, too,
his Vision regards her, addressing her "Courteous
Queen, Matchless Mother, Merriest Maid"
(ll. 432-434). In addition Rolle counsels meditation on the wretchedness of this life and the
joys of heaven. And when devotion fails he
says:

> I hold it than moste sekyre vn-to þe for to say the
> Pater Noster & þine Ave Marie. . . . For þat es ever-
> more a sekyr standard þat will noghte faile.[55]

and one thinks ahead to the later plaint, in
Pearl, "Thou never knewest Pater nor Creed"
(485). The chapter ends with an exhorta-
tion against curious seeking into the ways and
dispositions of God. It sounds curiously like a
voice, of which a later poet has caught and trans-
figured the echo. His conclusion is:

> Lord, mad are they that 'gainst Thee strive,
> or 'gainst Thy pleasure proffer aught. (ll. 1199-1200)

---

[55] *English Prose Treatises of Richard Rolle de Hampole,*
edited from Robert Thornton's MS., E. E. T. S., London, 1866-
1921, Vol. XI, pp. 38-43.

Rolle's *Fire of Love,* the date of composition of which is unknown, Englisht in 1435 by Richard Misyn, the prior of the Carmelite monastery at Lincoln, is a more complete and penetrating text upon mysticism, upon the life of union with God. Undoubtedly it bears the closest relation to the *Imitation of Christ.* The chapter titles are in most cases similar and in many cases almost identical, as: "Differens betwix Godis lufars & Þe worldis," and "The Proofs of a True Lover." This again substantiates the statement that an intense and mystical life flourished and was thoroughly articulate in fourteenth century England. Expression was as inevitable in this as in other fields of rich and active mental life and that expression comprises a very considerable, if heretofore neglected, literature. In this closely wrought work of a hundred and more pages, Rolle lays down the preliminary fact that all men must turn to God and away from earth to taste the sweetness of God's love. His prologue is the frankest of apologies. He marvels, he says, more than he can "shewe" at the fire of sensible devotion, of spiritual love with which he was first drawn to God. And because he himself is busy with love, and wishes others to be so stirred, he calls his volume the "byrnnyng of lufe." He offers his book, he says, not to phi-

losophers and wise men, but to the simple and
the unlearned—the "boystus & vntaght." He
expresses no doubt as to an audience, nor is he
apologetic for the unmixed spirituality of its con-
tents. He promises to the lovers of God tribulations in this life, bids them love rather than
know (the dear old scholastic controversy!) for
they shall rest in Christ and find incredible joy
in the Blessed Virgin, the "blist maydin." When
the soul loves God, he says, it feels heat, love,
and sweetness; such lovers are like the topaz,
precious and dear, pure as gold, clear as heaven,
and fairest of all things to behold—a suggestion
of jewel comparison for *Pearl*. Then follows
a personal account of his own conversion; its
beginning three years "except three or four
months" previous, the sensible and ecstatic experience of heavenly music eight or nine months
later, his own inspiration to song, and his com-
pleted conversion, the process of his spiritual
progress having been four years and three
months; "fiyre ere and about iii monethes I
had." The "history of his case" might serve
as a model in the most modern of hospital records.
One does not question the foundation for such
writing nor the understanding of the audience to
whom it was addressed. If Michael Wiggles-
worth's *Day of Doom* signifies specific things

about the New England of 1650 and the *Spoon River Anthology* certain other conditions of America's Middle West of 1910, the *Fire of Love* quite as authentically registers the spiritual temperature of England six centuries before. Its author sighs for death as the only means of union with his Beloved Whom he calls upon to kiss him with the kiss of His mouth. One does not speak thus to the untaught of a material-minded age, nor address the faithful soul as the spouse of Christ, "spows of Ihesu criste—cristis gardyn."

Out of the ecstatic praise of love, of which the second part of his book is one breathless canticle, one might select his contemplation of "heavenly misterys," opened, he tells us, "in meditacion"; for which he says the soul gladly "suffyrs adversite þat happyns, for in Ioy of everlastynge lufe swetly it restys." Or as the *Pearl* poet says:

> Me pleased it ill to be out cast
> So suddenly from that fair realm
> "O Pearl," quoth I, "of rich renown,
> if the tale be verily true,
> that thou thus farest, in garland gay,
> So well is me in this dungeon dire,
> that thou art pleasing to that Prince!" (ll. 1177-1188)

In the constraint of remaining upon earth the lover consummates his union thus: "O swete Ihesu, Þi lufe in me I bynde with a knot vnabyll to be lowsyd." Rolle bewails the necessity of living longer upon earth, but in complete detachment of soul and affections he sets his heart firmly in Christ in burning love until he shall be united to Him in heaven. Here is, truly, one of the most introspective of spiritual autobiographies, the record of a soul burning, consumed with such ardor as never overwhelmed and prostrated a knight of courtly love.

Ego Dormio et Cor Meum Vigilat, addressed to a nun for whom he probably acted as spiritual director, continues the theme of the heavenly Lover and concludes with a lyrical rhymed Song of Love "that thou shalt delight in when thou art loving Jesus Christ." *A Commandment of Love to God,* addressed to Margery of Hampole, elaborates the three degrees of love enumerated in his earlier instructions to her, the *Form of Perfect Living.* His *Meditatio de Passione Domine,* based on a translation from St. Bonaventure, is aflame with the same fire of spiritual ardor. Many other works are attributed to Richard Rolle; among them the *Prick of Conscience* is the grimmest and most uncompromising. If the *Fire of Love* is addressed to Infinite Love, this is written to Infinite Justice, a terrible reality to contemplate. It keeps company with Robert Mannyng's *Handlyng Synne* and the *Ayenbite of Inwyte* by "dan Michelis of Northgate."

The writings of Rolle are essential in the literature of his century. Thirty years younger than Chaucer, he was, like him, the leader of a distinct school, the promoter of a tremendous spiritual tradition which had its English beginnings with St. Hilda and Whitby and its latest significant expression in Francis Thompson. One traces it century by century through Cædmon and Cynewulf, through the anchoresses of Tarent, through parts of Spenser, Hooker, Baker, through Herbert and Vaughan and Crashaw, through Donne and Foxe, Cowley, Browne, Bunyan, Blake, Keble, DeVere, the Rossettis, and Patmore. It is a significant current and one responsible for more nuances and intangibilities in our literature than we guess. What Chaucer was to narrative and metrical art of this period, Rolle was to its spiritual expression. Each had his followers; each precipitated a deal of writing in imitation of his own; each awoke a world of echoes. Commonly, we have remembered Chaucer and have made the century synonymous with him. As Gower, Lydgate, Occleve, Bar-

bour, Henryson received his mantle, without indeed, its magic; so Rolle, too, left to a distinct
group of followers his legacy of mystical thought
and mystical expression.

Walter Hilton was to him as Eliseus to Elias
and much more than Gower to Chaucer. His
Scale of Perfection, a long prose work, seems to
have been designed as a book of spiritual direction, devoted chiefly to the reformation of the
soul to the image of God. His *Epistle on Mixed
Life* is significant in that it is addressed to "a
devout man in temporal estate, how he sholde
rule him," and rests on a comparison of the active
with the contemplative life. That such a book
should be possible (and it was printed by Julian
Notary in 1507, de Worde in 1525 and 1533,
and Pynson in 1516) [56] is an index to the secular
temper of the time.

Of Angels' Song and *Proper Will,* whether
by Rolle or Hilton, repeat the familar themes,
conformity to the will of God, purity of soul, the
happiness of heaven. William Nassington is the
Lydgate of this spiritual group, with little origi-
nality or poetical faculty; a translator with a gift
of fluent verse which he adapted to the prose
works of Rolle.

---

[56] J. E. Wells, *Manual of the Writings in Middle English,*
New Haven, 1916, p. 461.

Two women stand out conspicuously in this mystical school of fourteenth century England, Margery Kempe of Lynn and Juliana of Norwich. Of Margery we know little beyond what is contained in a tiny manuscript in the Cambridge University Library, which was printed by Pepwell in 1521. *The Booke of Margery Kempe of Lynn* it is called and speaks the familiar language of the beloved and the Lover: "Good Lord I would be laid naked on a hurdle for Thy love," and "Daughter I must needs comfort thee, for now thou hast the right way to Heaven . . . he that dreadeth the shames of this world may not perfectly love God." [57]

From the long life of Juliana of Norwich there remains but the one quaint, exquisite volume, fruit of her face to face communion with God, her *Sixteen Revelations,* which are like an epitome of Rolle's voluminous treatises, the quintessence of mystical theology. Her own summary, in the last chapter, reads: "I desire oftentimes to learn what was our Lord's meaning. And fifteen years after and more, I was answered in ghostly understanding. Saying thus: 'Wouldst thou learn thy Lord's meaning in this thing? Learn it well: Love was His meaning. Who showed it thee? Love. What showed He thee? Love. Where-

---

[57] G. Robinson, *In a Mediæval Library,* London, 1918, p. 89.

fore showed it He? For love.' " [58]   What her
preparation for such perfect initiation was we do
not know.   Her "revelations" she says,

were shewed to a simple creature unlettered, the year
of our Lord 1373, the eighth day of May. Which creature [she continues] (had) afore desired three gifts of
God. The First was mind of His Passion; [a gift which
St. Gertrude asked for and received] the Second was
bodily sickness in youth, at thirty years of age; [Juliana
lived to be perhaps a hundred] the Third was to have
of God's gift three wounds.[59]

Her book reveals the fullness of God's answer
to her prayer.   She is probably the same Lady
Juliana who in 1393 was living in the parish of
Conisford, outside Norwich, where to-day are still
traces of a little cell.[60]   She had two predecessors,
Dame Agnes and Dame Elizabeth, and as many
successors, Dame Elizabeth and Dame Agnes
Edrygge, and in her own day was only one of a
number of souls who dared to set up walls between
themselves and the world, to die to all things
and themselves that they might live to God.
What else, after all, was the Quest of the Holy
Grail? [61]

---

[58] Juliana of Norwich, *Revelations of Divine Love,* London,
1923, p. 202.

[59] *Op. cit.,* p. 3.

[60] Blomerfield, *History of Norfolk,* Vol. IV, p. 81.

[61] *Anchorland,* a novel by Enid Dinnis, has Juliana of Nor-

Nothing could be more explicit and simple—
two qualities that have everywhere characterized
true mystical writers—than her exposition of her
infused knowledge of God. It was composed,
she says, first, of Christ's crowning with thorns;
second, the changing of the color of His face
in token of His passion; third, His identity with
all creation; fourth, His scourging; fifth, His
victory over the devil; sixth, the reward of
heaven; seventh, God's equal love for us in weal
and woe; eighth, the death of Christ; ninth, the
merits of Christ's passion; tenth, the love of
Christ's heart; eleventh, the vision of His mother;
twelfth, thirteenth, fourteenth, and fifteenth, the
infinite might, goodness, and wisdom of God; and
sixteenth, the relation of the "Blissful Trinity"
to our soul. It reads like Angela of Foligno's
eighteen steps toward the road of penance and
involves much the same experience. It is possible
that Dame Juliana knew her book. And she
has achieved a naïveté complete beyond the hopes
of lucidity in her management of material. Writing upon a subject for which human language at
its richest supplies a limited vocabulary and of
which the tongues of men speak haltingly, she

---

wich for its heroine, and represents rather faithfully, one
would think, the manner of her life before and after her
immurement, her activities, and her death.

quite calmly supplies the deficiencies with compounds to suit her need and to embody her thought.   The General-Man, the All-Man, Nature-Goodness, Nature-Soul, Nature-Love, Nature-Substance, Sense-Soul, Sense-Part are words that can work for their living and can yield a return of all the thought that is in them.   They are patterns in terminology for us moderns.   Our inventiveness has been all on the side of obscurity.

The manner of Juliana's "shewings" may best be illustrated by quotation.   And in making selections I have chosen such passages as most nearly resemble the matter of the *Pearl*.   Of God the Father and the Son she says:

Now sitteth not the Son on earth in wilderness, but He sittest in His noblest seat, which He made in Heaven most to His pleasing. . . . He standeth afore the Father even-right richly clad in blissful largeness, with a Crown upon His head of precious richness.

or as *Pearl* has it:

Before them proudly passed the Lamb.

    ·   ·   ·   ·   ·   ·

His robe most like to precious pearls.

    ·   ·   ·   ·   ·   ·

So wondrous white was His array,
Simple His looks, Himself so calm. (ll. 1110-1134)

For it was shewed that *we be His Crown*. . . . Now is the Spouse, God's Son, in peace with His loved Wife,

which is the Fair Maiden of Endless Joy. . . . And thus
I saw that God rejoiceth that He is our Father, and
God rejoiceth that He is our Mother, and God rejoiceth
that He is our Very Spouse and our soul is His loved
Wife.[62]

This fits absolutely the *Pearl* poet's vision:

My spotless Lamb, Who can better all,

. . . . . .

chose me His bride, though all unfit
the Spousal might a while well seem,

. . . . . .

We all in bliss are Brides of the Lamb. (ll. 757-785)

So also does this picture of the Mother of God:

Fair and sweet is our Heavenly Mother in the sight
of our souls; precious and lovely are the Gracious Children in the sight of our Heavenly Mother, with mild-
ness and meekness, and all the fair virtues that belong
to children in nature.

She holdeth empire high o'er all;
and this displeaseth none of our host,
for she is Queen of Courtesy. (ll. 454-456)

And I understood none higher stature in this life than
childhood. . . . Thus I understood that all His blessed
children which be come out of Him by Nature shall be
brought again unto Him by grace.[63]

---

[62] Juliana of Norwich, *Revelations of Divine Love*, pp. 120-
121.

[63] *Op. cit.*, pp. 158-159.

This fits in again perfectly with the *Pearl* poet's vision of a child, as also his exposition of grace. The following is equally pertinent:

> Enough from out that well there flowed,
> Blood and water, from wound so wide;
>
> .   .   .   .   .   .
>
> And ransomed us from second death;
>
> .   .   .   .   .   .
>
> All is restored in one fair hour.
> The grace of God is great enough. (ll. 649-660)

And in this time I saw a body lying on the earth, which body shewed heavy and horrible. . . . And suddenly out of this body sprang a full fair creature, a little child, fully shapen and formed, nimble and lively, whiter than a lily, which swiftly glided up into heaven. And the swollenness of the body betokeneth great wretchedness of our deadly flesh, and the littleness of the Child betokeneth the cleanness of purity in soul.

The *Pearl* poet uses the same comparison:

> no man might win His realm
> save he came thither as a child;
>
> .   .   .   .   .   .
>
> Harmless, undefiled, and true. (ll. 722-725)

In the presence of such richness of imagery, such multiplicity of figures to betoken states of soul and of divinity, one does not feel that a lone, lost pearl within a grassy arbor is so solitary an instance of spiritual exposition in metaphor.

Blessed Juliana's visions were not all of heaven, nor were her revelations entirely of future bliss. God showed her two manners of sickness, she says: "the one is impatience or sloth" in bearing suffering of whatever kind unwillingly, the other is "despair and doubtful dread," both of which are confessed by the author of *Pearl*. Her sixteenth revelation is ecstatic; heaven is the end of all vision whether it be that of a Florentine poet or an English anchoress.

And then our Lord opened my spiritual eye and shewed me my soul in the midst of my heart. [Very like Angela of Foligno's two divisions is this.] I saw the Soul so large as it were an endless world, and as it were a blissful kingdom . . . the place that Jesus taketh in our Soul He shall never remove it . . . for in us is His homeliest home and His endless dwelling. . . . Glad and joyous and sweet is the love-longing; and He willeth that our Soul be in glad cheer to His meed.

This is quite like the *Pearl*:

Delight that there His coming brought
too much it were to tell thereof,

.   .   .   .   .   .

then glory and glee pour'd forth anew;
all sang to laud that gladsome Jewel. (ll. 1117-1128)

No writer upon a secular theme proceeds with more certainty and direction of aim, with more

calm command of material and method, with more
clearness of vision. The *Revelations* of Juliana
are not the vague records of a visionary; they rest
on an ethic, a code, a recognized relation as positive as that of *Troilus and Cressida* and in the
same century may signify more.

One might stop at the sayings of John Morton,
an Augustinian canon of York whose writings are
preserved in manuscript in the Bodelian Library,
and find the same spirit of a native son in the land
of mystical promise. One might go through the
wealth of unidentified or anonymous spiritual writing of the period, in prose and verse. Among the
hundreds of religious lyrics, those addressed to
Christ or the Blessed Virgin are the most varied
and personal and those motivated by mystical
fervor and understanding are the best. Christ,
the heavenly Lover, and Mary, the Queen of
Heaven, are persistent themes of Middle English
lyrics. Those of William Herbert, a Franciscan
monk who died about 1330, are possessed of a
fine, not to say a martial vigor. They are the
marching lyrics of the Church militant—a rendering of the *Vexilla Regis prodeunt,* the *Kynges
Banneres beth forth y-led,* English versions of the
Latin *Gloria laus et honor tibi sit,* of the Palm
Sunday processional, of Jeremias' *Populi mi, quid
feci tibi* of Good Friday, of the *Veni Creator*

Spiritus and the *Ave Maris Stella*. Among anonymous poems there is the deeply mystical *Thou, wommun, boute vere,* which considers the involved and metaphysical relation of Mary as Mother of God, her Father and Brother, and sister and mother of the poet. It is such a tangle of perplexities as one can imagine might have occurred to the *Pearl* poet, also. *Gabriel from Eveneking* is a free translation following the stanza and form of the *Angelus ad Virginem,* mentioned by Chaucer in the Miller's Tale. It might be not an impossible task to trace at least some instinct of the mystic in Chaucer, though I suspect that Dan Geoffrey would be horrified at even the mention of such an attempt.

As has already been said, the religious lyrics completely overshadowed the secular in number; there were hundreds of them in every form of stanza and meter, on every aspect of piety and devotion. There were the quaintest of lullabies and the most sorrowful of laments, alliterative "Salutations to Our Lady," and "Forebodings of the Passion." Poetic delicacy and spiritual beauty many times met and kissed in lines such as these:

> I sing of a maiden
> That matchless is:
> King of all kings
> Was her Son, i-wis.

He came all so still
Where His mother was
As dew in April
That falleth on grass:
He came all so still
To His mother's bower
As dew in April
That falleth on flower:
He came all so still
Where His mother lay
As dew in April
That formeth on spray.
Mother and maiden
Was ne'er none but she:
Well may such a lady
God's mother be.[64]

The skill of the poet as well as the magnitude of his theme not infrequently expanded these religious poems to considerable length. The "Quatrefoil of Love" is an excellent example. It is found in a fifteenth century quarto; and is a poem of forty stanzas of thirteen lines each, the first eight of thirteen syllables, the ninth of two, and the other four of six. The rime scheme is likewise involved; ababababcdddc. In form it is not unlike the twelve-line stanza of *Pearl* with its ababababbcbc rime. The situations at the open-

---

[64] M. G. Segar, "God's Mother," *A Mediæval Anthology,* New York, 1915, p. 59.

ings of the two poems are almost identical; the time is summer—beloved season of the early lyrists—there is the same setting of trees and grass and flowers, with the disconsolate and passive poet awaiting the event. In this poem it is a revelation of true love; but true love the poet identifies in the eighth stanza with God; its manifestations he traces through the creation, the annunciation, the nativity of Christ, His baptism, passion, and death, resurrection, and ascension. The first seven stanzas are given to an exposition of "trew lufe," the last fourteen develop its practical application to the life of man and his corresponding obligations. The poem has not the perfection of plan that one finds in the *Pearl* but in intention approaches it. Also, it displays the same devotion to the Scripture, particularly to the New Testament, although differing in selection of material.

There are two much closer parallels in matter. The parable of the laborers, so elaborately explained by the maiden in *Pearl*, is related in a poem of about 1310, *Of a mon Mathew Thohte*. It is only five stanzas long, twelve lines each, with an aabaabccbccb rime; the b lines of three and the others of four stresses. The first four stanzas relate the parable with much direct discourse and the fifth supplies the story to the poet's own restless state [65]—a situation, taken all in all, not unlike a miniature *Pearl.* The second is *The Apocalypse of St. John,* with a commentary, formerly attributed erroneously to Wycliffe. It is preserved in sixteen manuscripts, in groups of from three to five verses, each group followed by its commentary, and should be considered in relation to the sixteenth division of *Pearl,* the exposition of the New Jerusalem.[66]

The mystical element that one misses in all of these is abundantly present in "A Luv Ron," of Friar Thomas of Hales, "Quia Amore Langueo," and "Of Clean Maidenhood." Professor Gollancz has already called attention to this last poem in his introduction to his latest edition of *Pearl* (1921).

The author was no doubt acquainted with English poets, his contemporaries and predecessors. He would have been attracted to the writing of Hampole and other mystics, and also to the English homilies on Holy Maidenhood, with note: compare especially the thirteenth century alliterative homily, "Holi Maidenhad."

A closer comparison of all three poems with *Pearl* will be made in the detailed discussion of that text; for the general purpose of background it will suffice to note here that "Luv Ron"

---

[65] J. E. Wells, *Manual of the Writing on Middle English,* p. 409.

[66] *Op. cit.,* p. 409.

has for theme Christ, the perfect Lover, and virginity, "the fire-begotten gem" "that healeth love's wound"; "Quia Amore Langueo" pictures Christ, the lover seeking His spouse, man's soul; while "Clean Maidenhood" again repeats the theme of chastity and the gem of virginity.

The student has the habit of looking for what he wants, perhaps to the exclusion of many more apparent things. A background, a tradition, and an environment of mystical literature were the things devoutly to be wished in this instance. The existence of all three has been pretty clearly demonstrated; complete exploitation would require volumes. And in this summary of mediæval spiritual writing a number of things have become evident. First of all, the mystic, while living entirely by the clock of eternity, is intensely a man of his own time. Bernard was a Crusader; Bonaventure, a statesman; Ramon Lull, a soldier and a scientist; Catherine of Siena, a diplomat; and Walter Hilton, adviser to the mother of the first Tudor. Most of the men among the group here considered held chairs of philosophy at the University of Paris, Cologne, Oxford, or other Universities of their day. What they wrote should, for this reason, be fairly representative of the general spirit of their times.

Without exception, they wrote expositions of

the spiritual or interior life; many of them wrote these in autobiographical form; many of them employed dialogue, with the Soul and Christ, or Eternal Wisdom, or a Vision as dramatis personæ; all of them record repeated experiences in spiritual dryness and interior desolation; all of them counsel abandonment to God; all of them propose the passion of Christ and the intercession of the Blessed Virgin as sources of spiritual consolation; all hold out the vision and hope of heaven not only as the object of all spiritual desire but as the comfort for all spiritual "blues." Equally, all of them regard the relation of Christ to the soul as that of the Lover to His beloved; the friendship is never Platonic or unemotional or sweetly pious; it is always of the most outspoken and passionate ardor. It is essentially nuptial. Conspicuous works embodying all of these characteristics are:

The *Eighteen Spiritual Steps* of Angelo of Foligno; *The Book of the Lover and the Beloved,* by Ramon Lull; the *Little Book of Eternal Wisdom,* by Henry Suso; the *Fire of Love,* attributed to Richard Rolle; the *Revelations of Divine Love,* by Juliana of Norwich; the *Imitation of Christ,* by Thomas à Kempis. All of these facts furnish excellent justification and support for a spiritual interpretation of *Pearl.*

CHAPTER IV

A REINTERPRETATION OF "PEARL"

1. The Significance of the Introductory and Concluding Stanzas

THE *Pearl* I take to be a very beautifully wrought account of an experience in interior desolation. It opens with a real case of spiritual "blues," followed by a consideration of God's grace, elaborated by a number of natural and characteristic digressions and brought to a perfectly consistent climax, the contemplation of heaven. It ends with the poet's complete resignation to the will of God, which is both the ideal cure for his malady and the ideal conclusion for the poem. The fact that autobiography dons the lovely robe of symbolism and walks incognito in allegory may suggest resemblances to the *Romaunt of the Rose,* the only secular poem with which it has been seriously compared; it points much more significantly to kinship with the great body of religious writing, prose and poetry, already indicated in part. Spirituality, even more than love, has always spoken a symbolic language, and without parable its speech almost does not exist. I believe that the author of the *Pearl* was a religious who, if not young himself, was recording the experience of one young in religion. As to wife, and child, and bereavement, I say that there was no wife, there was no two-year-old daughter and consequently no bereavement—"there is no Marjorie Daw."

In the first place, I think that the poem should be understood in the light of its beginning and its end. All apocalyptic utterances must be so interpreted, whether it be the prophetic books of the *Scripture,* the *Koran,* or the *Divine Comedy.* Now, the first five stanzas tell of the loss of a precious pearl, "wyth-outen spot," which I take to be a state of soul, that spiritual sweetness and interior consolation already described. It is, as I have explained, a characteristic of the early period of religious life. The poet states his case thus:

I

Pearl all-pleasing, prince's treasure,
Too chastely set in gold so pure!
From out the Orient, I aver,
Ne'er proved I pearl its precious peer.
So round, so royal where ever ranged
so sweetly small, so wondrous smooth;
where e'er I judged of joyous gems,
I placed my Pearl apart, supreme.

I lost it—in a garden—alas!
Through grass to ground 'twas gone from me.
I pined, by Severing Love despoil'd
Of Pearl mine own, without a spot.

II

There, in that spot, since hence it sped,
Oft have I watch'd, wanting that gem
that was wont to vanquish woe,
and raise my hap and all my weal.
It doth but pierce my heart with pain.
my breast in bale but boil and burn;
yet ne'er me seem'd so sweet a song
as that still hour let steal to me.
Yea, many a thought to me flow'd there,
Musing its charms so clad in clay.
O! earth! thou marrest a merry theme,—
Pearl mine own, without a spot.

III

From spot where such rich treasure wastes
fragrant spice must needs spring forth;
blossoms white and blue and red
shine there full sheer against the sun.
Flower and fruit shall know no flaw
where it down drave to earth's dark mold;
for from dead grain each blade must grow,
no wheat were else brought ever home.
Each good from good is aye begun;
so seemly a seed can never fail;
ne'er fragrant spice shall cease to spring
from that precious Pearl without a spot.

IV

Unto the spot I picture forth
I enter'd into that garden green;
'twas August, at a festal tide,
when corn is cut with keen-edg'd hook.
The mound my Pearl had roll'd adown
with herbs was shadow'd, beauteous, bright,—
gilvers, ginger, and gromwell-seed,
and peonies powder'd all about
But if the sight was sweet to see,
fair, too, the fragrance floating thence,
where dwelleth that glory, I wot full well,
my precious Pearl without a spot.

V

Before that spot my hands I clasp'd,
for care full cold that seized on me;
a senseless moan dinned in my heart,
though Reason bade me be at peace.
I plain'd my Pearl, imprison'd there,
with wayward words that fiercely fought;
though Christ Himself me comfort show'd,
my wretched will worked aye in woe.
I fell upon that flowery plot;
such fragrance flash'd into my brain,
I slid into a slumber-swoon
o'er that precious Pearl without a spot.

Here is a situation, significant in every detail.
First of all, the poet has lost a pearl in a garden;
has been despoiled of his jewel by severing love.
He seeks it in the spot where he lost it; and

despite his consciousness of loss, he feels a sweetness steal upon him there as he meditates upon
the charm, the "color" of his lost gem. He thinks
that from the spot where his pearl lies, fairest
flowers, richest grain, sweetest spices must hence-
forth grow. He then bethinks himself to say
that he was overtaken by this calamity in August,
on a feast day, to be precise. And here, the sight
of the spot where he had lost his jewel over-
whelms him in spite of reason; he rebels, and
though comforted by Christ, is still unreconciled.

The possibilities here are two: the writer either
refers to a person or he does not. As Professor
Schofield has pointed out, he nowhere gives evidence that he has a person in mind; indeed, his
description of the *Pearl* becomes almost absurd
when applied to a young girl. Obviously he does
not mean an actual pearl. If he has in mind a
state of soul, as I maintain, the details are to be
interpreted thus. The poet has lost a thing of
sensible sweetness and beauty to him; something
which he would compare in loveliness and value
with an orient pearl, of singular and unique value
in his life. Love has taken it from him, he
realizes, and yet he must mourn his loss. Desolation has, for the time, taken the place of interior
consolation. God has deprived him of this, he
plainly recognizes; nevertheless, he cannot refrain

from lament. The condition is, as I have said,
typical. Blessed Henry Suso, writing in Germany
at this very time, says:

A preacher once stood, after matins, before a crucifix,
and complained from his heart to God that he could
not meditate properly on His torments and passion, and
that this was very bitter for him, in as much as, up to
that hour, he had in consequence suffered so much. And,
as he thus stood with his complaint, his interior senses
were wrapt to an unusual exaltation, in which he was
very speedily and clearly enlightened.[67]

Blessed Juliana in her anchorhold at Norwich,
records a similar experience:

And after this He shewed a sovereign ghostly pleasance
in my soul. I was fulfilled with the everlasting sureness, mightily sustained without any painful dread. This
feeling was so glad and so ghostly that I was in all peace
and in rest, that there was nothing in earth that should
have grieved me.

This lasted but a while, and I was turned and left
to myself in heaviness, and weariness of my life, and
irksomeness of my soul, that scarcely I could have patience to live. There was no comfort nor none ease
to me but faith, hope, and charity; and these I had in
truth but little in feeling.[68]

---

[67] Blessed Henry Suso, *Little Book of Eternal Wisdom*, London, 1910, p. 20.

[68] Juliana, Anchoress at Norwich, *Revelations of Divine Love*,
London, 1923, p. 34.

A hundred years earlier St. Gertrude had written:

The grace makes me know further, by frequent revelations, that the soul, dwelling in the body of frail humanity, is darkened in the same manner as a person who stands in a narrow space, and is surrounded on all sides by a vapor exhaling from a cooking vessel. And when the body is afflicted by any evil, the part which suffers is to the soul as a beam from the sun which enlightens the air, and from which it receives a marvellous clearness; therefore the heavier one's sufferings are, the purer is the light the soul receives. But afflictions and trials of the heart in humility, patience, and other virtues impart the greatest luster to the soul, as they touch it more keenly, efficaciously, and intimately.

Thanks be to Thee, O Lover of men, that Thou hast sometimes led me by this means to patience! But alas!— and a thousand times, alas! how seldom have I listened to the counsels or rather, how seldom have I done what I ought to have done! [69]

Evidence, this, that the *Pearl* poet had illustrious company in his rebellion no less than in his joy. The Pearl itself seems not, from the details of description, to refer to a girl; it can easily be a figure of the soul, virginity, chastity, salvation—or any dear virtue—and has yielded all of those meanings in the interpretations of

[69] *The Life and Revelations of Saint Gertrude,* London, pp. 99-100.

the Scripture parable: "The kingdom of heaven is like to a merchant seeking good pearls. Who, when he had found one pearl of great price, went his way, and sold all that he had, and bought it." St. Matthew xiii, 45, 46. I am quite aware that poets have paid tribute to women under this figure, notably in the Middle Ages to the Blessed Virgin, but never with such unlikely details as, "so rounde . . . so smal, so smothe her sydes were." The employment of jewel-comparisons among spiritual writers is universal, elaborate, and often far-fetched. Here are three from the *Ancren Riwle*: "Salue crux que in corpore Christi dedicata es, et ex membris ejus tanquam margaritis ornata. Hail, O Cross, who in the body of Christ wast dedicated, and with his limbs adorned, as with pearls" (18). "This precious stone is Jesus Christ; a faithful stone, and full of all might, above all precious stones" (134). "Treasure is a good deed, which is compared to heaven. . . . Look, here it is; red gold and white silver enough, and precious jewels" (150-153).

Blessed Henry Suso writes of himself:

Once upon a time, as he sat at table in the guest house, a brother insulted him with scornful talk. Upon which the Servitor (Suso) turned towards him very lovingly, and smiled upon him, as though he had just received a precious jewel from him.[70]

The religious lyrics of this and the preceding century show the same richness of jewel imagery. One finds it elaborately developed in "The Luve Ron" of about 1244-1250.

> Sweeter than any flower art thou
> When keeping well thy castle.
>
> It is a fire-begotten gem,
> The finest 'neath high Heaven;
> It healeth love wounds all: before
> All others be it chosen:
> . . . . . .
> This precious gem of which I tell,
> Virginity they name it;
> Its price is great, for of all gems
> The noblest I proclaim it.
> . . . . . .

Here follows a comparison with all precious stones familiar to mediæval lapidarists, and the poem continues:

> O maid, so as I've told thee
> This gem within thy tower
> Is brighter far a hundred fold
> Than all these stones so fair:

---

[70] *The Life of Blessed Henry Suso,* by himself, London, p. 111.

It's fashioned e'en in Heaven's gold
It's full of love the finest:
Whoso' shall keep it fast, shall gleam
In Heaven with light divinest.[71]

From this it is evident that the pearl, or any
other gem, as a figure of spirituality was part
of the metaphorical language employed by religious writers in this age; it was neither unusual
nor ambiguous; it conveyed to the readers precisely the qualities desired: beauty, virtue, rarity.
Neither religious nor secular writing shows any
general tendency to symbolize childhood or the
individual child under this figure nor, indeed, any
single instance of it.   If the *Pearl* is an elegy
for a little girl, it is unique in the history of
English literature until the sixteenth century; if
it is an allegory of a spiritual condition, it is a
part of the mystical writing and tradition of the
century which gave it being.

The garden in which the Pearl was lost may
be a mediæval convention, the familiar setting that
one finds in the opening stanzas of the "Quatrefoil of Love":

---

[71] *An Old English Miscellany,* Early English Text Society,
edited by J. M. Cowper, London, 1871, pp. 97, 98.
  The poem is attributed to Friar Thomas of Hales, and
has been given this modern form by the Reverend Cuthbert,
O. S. F. C. It is included in Mary Segar's Mediæval Anthology, London, 1915, p. 59.

In a morwenyng of Maye whenne medowes salle spryng
Blomes and blossomes of brighte coloures:
Also I went by a welle: on my playing:
Thurghe a mery orcherde bed and myne howres:
The birdes one bewes bigone for to synge:
And bowes for to burgeone and beld to the bo(ures):
Was I warre of a mayde that made mournyng:
Sekande and syghand amang those floures;
So swete.
Scho made mournynge ynoughe:
Hie wepynge dide me woughe:
Undir a tree I me droughe:
Hir wille wolde I wete.[72]

Or it may be taken figuratively, as in "Quia
Amore Langueo":

> In a valey of this restles mynde
> I sowghte in mounteyne & in myde,
>
> .   .   .   .   .   .
>
> Trustyinge a trewe love for to fynde.
> Vpon on hil than y took hede;
> A voyce y herde & neer y yede
> In hugh dolour complaynynge tho,
> "Se, dere soule, how my sidis blede,
> Quia amore langueo." [73]

It may be the herb-garden of a monastery,
fair and fragrant with such plants as one would

---

[72] The "Quatrefoil of Love," an alliterative religious poem included in *An English Miscellany*, F. J. Furnivall, Oxford, 1901, p. 112.

[73] "Quia Amore Langueo," included in *Political, Religious, and Love Poems*, E. E. T. S., F. J. Furnivall, London, 1903, p. 180.

find there: gillyflowers, ginger, gromwell-seed, peonies. It is not a graveyard; it has nothing of the appearance, the atmosphere, or the conventions of a cemetery. It is twice called definitely a garden, "on erbere," and is described as such.

The only suggestion of death that one can take from the setting of the poem occurs in connection with lines 29-32:

> Flower and fruit shall know no flaw
> where it down drave to earth's dark mould;
> for from dead grain each blade must grow,
> no wheat were else brought ever home.

The reference here is perfectly evident; it points directly back to the Gospel of St. John, xii, 24: "Unless the grain of wheat falling into the ground die, itself remaineth alone. But if it die, it bringeth forth much fruit. He that loveth his life shall lose it, and he that hateth his life in this world, keepeth it unto life eternal." Or again, the figure is used with force and consistency in the First Epistle of St. Paul to the Corinthians, xv, 36: "Senseless man, that which thou sowest is not quickened, except it die first. And that which thou sowest, thou sowest not the body that shall be; but bare grain, as of wheat." These passages can be interpreted as direct expositions of the resurrection of the body; indeed, the excerpt from St. Paul is a part of his great discourse on that subject. However, their application can be extended to include the glorification of any state, condition, or desire, through the death of its transitory, natural, mortal part. The flowers of the most substantial virtues, to keep the figure, grow from the graves of renunciation, self-conquest, spiritual bereavement. If, through constant and unremitting effort, I subdue, or conquer, or kill a certain intellectual pride that I recognize in myself, I find that, as a consequence, I have achieved a real sense of my own capabilities—which is humility. If I hold in check my natural impetuosity of spirit, I acquire the opposite virtue of resignation. So, from the death of every fault or imperfection arises the opposite virtue or perfection. This seems to be the application of the scriptural reference here because the line following reads: "Each good from good is aye begun." There is no allusion to the glory, or the transformation, by resurrection, of some beloved dead. As the action of the poem takes place chiefly in the poet's mind and in dream, the importance of the Arcadian setting is reduced. Personally, I regard it as referring to the cloister garden of the enclosure in which the poet lived. The religious state is generally regarded as the Lord's vineyard or garden: "The harvest indeed is great but the laborers are few. Pray ye therefore the Lord of the harvest, that he send forth laborers into his harvest." St. Matthew, ix, 37-38. The author of the *Ancren Riwle* says to his spiritual daughters: "Ye are young trees planted in God's orchard" (p. 287).

The poet's loss is a more important consideration. He recognizes that he has been "despoiled by Severing Love." Professor Gollancz capitalizes the words; he understands the lines to mean that God has taken the Pearl. This would be true if the poet was lamenting the death of a daughter. But take his loss to be of spiritual sweetness and behold the parallels. Suso says in Chapter ix of his *Little Book of Eternal Wisdom*:

The Servant: Lord, all has been explained to my heart's satisfaction, except one thing. In truth, Lord, when a soul is quite exhausted with yearning after Thee and the sweet caresses of Thy presence, then Lord, art Thou silent and sayest not a word. O Lord! ought not this to grieve my heart, that Thou, my tender Lord, Thou who art my only one love, and the sole desire of my heart shouldst yet behave Thyself so strangely, and in such a way hold Thy peace? . . . Alas! Lord, may I venture to say that Thou shouldst be a little more favorable to such poor affectionate hearts as pine and languish

for Thee, as breathe out so many an unfathomable sigh
to Thee, as look up so yearningly to Thee, crying aloud
from their very hearts, Return to us, O Lord! and
speaking and reasoning with themselves thus: Have we
cause to think that we have angered Him, and that He
will forsake us? Have we cause to think that He will
not give us His loving presence back again, so that we
may affectionately embrace Him with the arms of our
hearts and press Him to our bosoms till all our sorrow
vanish? Lord, all this Thou knowest and hearest, and
yet Thou art silent!

Again, in his *Life* (p. 40), he writes:

At first for a long time the Servitor was, as it were,
spoiled by God with heavenly consolations; and he was so
eager after them, that all subjects of contemplation which
had reference to the Divine Nature were a delight to
him; whereas, when he should have meditated on our
Lord's suffering, and sought to imitate Him in them,
this seemed to him a thing hard and bitter. He was
once severely rebuked by God for this, and it was said
to him: Knowest thou not that I am the door through
which all true friends of God must press in, if they
would attain to true bliss? Thou must break thy way
through My suffering Humanity, if thou wouldst verily
and indeed arrive at My naked Divinity. The Servitor
was struck with consternation at this, and it was a hard
saying to him; nevertheless, he commenced meditating
upon it, much though it went against him, and he began
to learn what till then he knew not, and he gave himself
up to practice it with detachment.

Juliana says in her seventh Revelation (p. 35):

This vision was shewed me, according to mine understanding, (for) that it is speedful to some souls to feel
on this wise: sometime to be in comfort, and sometime to fail and to be left to themselves. God willeth
that we know that He keepeth us even alike secure in
woe and in weal. And for profit of man's soul, a man
is sometime left to himself; although sin is not always
the cause: for in this time I sinned not wherefore I
should be left to myself—for it was so sudden. Also I
deserved not to have this blessed feeling. But freely
our Lord giveth when He will; and suffereth us [to be]
in woe sometime. And both is one love.

Thomas à Kempis, in the ninth chapter of the
second book of the *Imitation of Christ*, draws
this picture of a man in want of all comfort:

It is not hard to despise all human comfort when we
have divine. But it is much, very much to be able to
want all comfort, both human and divine; and to be
willing to bear this interior banishment for God's honor,
and to seek one's self in nothing, nor to think of one's
own merit. What great thing is it, if thou be cheerful
and devout when grace comes? . . .

But a true lover of Christ, and a diligent pursuer of
virtue, does not hunt after comfort, nor seek such sensible
sweetnesses: but is rather willing to bear strong trials
and hard labors for Christ.

Therefore when God gives spiritual comfort, receive
it with thanksgiving; but know that it is the bounty of
God, not thy merit. . . .

When comfort shall be taken away from thee, do not presently despair, but wait with humility and patience for the heavenly visit; for God is able to restore thee a greater consolation.

This is no new thing, nor strange to those who have experienced the ways of God; for in the great saints and ancient prophets there has always been this kind of variety. . . .

When I am forsaken by grace and left in my own poverty . . . at such a time, there is no better remedy than patience and leaving myself to the will of God.

The extract reads like a summary of the poem; the experience cited is identical with that related in the opening stanzas, as is also the reaction. One might almost be a paraphrase, an expansion of the other. The subtraction of spiritual sweetness is, as I have said, a very common experience and is always recognized by the initiated as a manifestation of God's love.

The poet sought his pearl where he had lost it, that is, in the condition and place of his former life. The lines here imply an expectation of the return of his treasure. He would hardly visit the grave of a child with such a hope; and he does, indeed, experience, in spite of his burning grief, a consolation like the sweetness of a song. The ravishment of heavenly music, one remembers, was the second distinct

experience of Richard Rolle in the process of his
conversion.   Likewise, John Ruysbroeck makes
celestial melody the fifth step in *Love's Gradatory* (p. 235):

> The first method of Celestial Song is love of God
> and men . . . the second . . . is unpretentious Hu-
> mility . . . the third consists in renouncing self-will and
> everything belonging to self, abandoning all to the most
> dear will of God and bearing submissively all He sees
> fit to impose.

Blessed Henry Suso used at break of day "to
fall at once on his knees, and salute the rising
morning star, heaven's gentle Queen," and he did
not merely say these words, but he accompanied
them with a "sweet still melody in his soul."
One does not kneel at a grave with a song in his
heart, ordinarily, nor could the poet here have
done so if his grief were bereavement—his own
word for it.   This record of music from other
contemporary mystics suggests to us the nice precision of detail in the *Pearl* poet's autobiography,
as also the sweetness of its meaning.

In the next stanza, he foregoes grief and becomes philosophical.   He figures that his loss is
not quite absolute; from a spot enriched by his
pearl a wealth of treasure, of lovely blossoms,
and richest spices must surely spring.   Fragrant

spices shall never cease to spring up here, he
says, with emphasis and repetition. Waiving for
the moment the absence of this idea from mediæval poetry on death, we may consider the prev-
alence of the figure of spices as typical of virtue,
especially such as one acquired by suffering, a
grace preservative and sweet to the soul. The
Ancren Riwle contains a typical exposition of
it (pp. 373-379):

Let us now say something of bitterness internal; for,
of these two bitternesses (external and internal) ariseth
sweetness, even in this world, and not in heaven only.

As I said just now that Nicodemus brought oint-
ments wherewith to anoint our Lord, even so, the three
Marys brought precious spices wherewith to anoint his
body. Take good heed now, my dear sisters; three
Marys denote three bitternesses. . . . This we see that
in every state bitterness prevails: first, in the beginning,
when we are reconciled to God . . . in the progress of
a good life . . . and in the last end. . . . But now,
observe here, my dear sisters, how after bitterness cometh
sweetness. Bitterness buyeth it, for, as the Gospel saith,
those three Marys brought sweet-smelling spices, to anoint
our Lord with. By spices, which are sweet, is to be
understood the sweetness of a devout heart. . . . Solo-
mon saith, "Esuriens, etc. If thou hungerest after the
sweet, thou must first, surely, eat of the bitter." In
the Canticles, "Ibo mihi, etc. I will go," saith God's
dear spouse, "to the hill of frankincense by the mountain
of myrrh." Observe: Which is the way to the sweetness of frankincense? By the myrrh of bitterness. And

again in the same love-book: "Who is she that goeth
up by the desert, as a pillar of smoke of aromatical spices,
of myrrh and frankincense?" Aromatic spices are composed of myrrh, and of frankincense. And myrrh he
placeth before, and frankincense cometh after. "Of aromatical spices, myrrh and frankincense." Now, some-
one complaineth that she cannot have sweetness—neither
God nor sweetness within. Let her not wonder, if she
is not Mary, for she must buy it with bitterness without;
but not with every bitterness, for some causeth to go
away from God, as every worldly pain which is not for
the health of the soul. Wherefore, in the Gospel it is
written of the three Marys in this manner, "That coming, they might anoint Jesus, but not going." These
three Marys, it is said, that is, these bitternesses, were
coming to anoint our Lord. Those sufferings are coming to anoint our Lord which we endure for His sake.

Another evidence that the spice garden was a
common figure for the soul, enriched with virtues,
carefully acquired and cultivated, occurs in Suso's
Book of Eternal Wisdom (p. 48). Eternal Wisdom, speaking to his servant, Suso, says of the
enervating effect of human presence to spiritual
sensitiveness:

What a hindrance, then, must not merely human
presence prove. . . . If thou hast still a doubt respect-
ing it, look around thee into the beautiful, fruitful vine-
yards which formerly were so delightful in their first
bloom. . . . How many a precious spice garden is there,
which, adorned with delightful gifts, was a heavenly

paradise . . . which . . . has become a garden of wild weeds.

Blessed Henry Suso describes such a spice garden as grew from sowings as bitter as the poet's own. Eternal Wisdom speaks thus to his servant:

Make up thy mind to a daring encounter, for thy heart, before thou shalt subdue thy nature, must often die, and thou must sweat the bloody sweat of anguish because of many a painful suffering under which I mean to prepare thee for Myself; for with red blossoms will I manure thy spice garden.[74]

It is no far cry from this to the poet's plight, and one may easily conclude that some such aromatic virtue, some such preserving grace and strength he looked for from the grave of his lost consolation.

In this mood of hope and resignation, he becomes more thoroughly practical and tells his reader that this thing befell him on a feast day in August. Two critics at least have cited the Feast of the Transfiguration and the Feast of the Assumption as days possibly intimated in " 'twas August, at a festal time." Both are excellent suggestions and highly probable, although one must remember that the matter of dating poems was somewhat of a convention in this

---

[74] Blessed Henry Suso, *Little Book of Eternal Wisdom,* London, 1910, p. 30.

century. One of Chaucer's poems is dated April,
two May, and the *House of Fame* is more specific, December tenth, which happens to be the
Feast of Loreto. Of the two dates suggested,
I should think that the Feast of the Assumption, August 15, is the one meant, for although
it is a feast of our Lady, while the other is of
our Lord, it is what is called a double of the
first class in the liturgy of the Church, is a holy
day of obligation, and has been, from earliest
Christian times, the most beloved of summer
festivals. One remembers, for instance, that in
Lufu's Will, [75] the Assumption of St. Mary is
the day on which his property was yearly to be
distributed. It is, however, a matter upon which
difference of opinion can hardly effect interpretation or amount to a scholarly heresy.

The last stanza of the introduction reiterates
the poet's lament; his grief persists, in spite of
reason, in spite of the comfort of Christ Himself. Exhausted by sorrow, but even more over-
powered by a fragrance which flashed upon him,
he fell "into a slumber swoon." Parallel quotations already cited illustrate how common is this
rebellion of affections against reason and the will
of God—the remonstrance that Suso makes in
his *Little Book of Eternal Wisdom* (p. 29):

---

[75] C. Sweet, *Oldest English Texts,* pp. 446-447.

But, Lord, this is a great marvel to my heart; I would needs seek . . . Thy sweetness, and Thou settest before me Thy bitterness; I would needs conquer, Thou teachest me to fight. Lord, what dost Thou mean?

One finds precisely the same bewildering loss and desolation in the *Revelations* of Juliana (pp. 34, 35):

And after this He shewed a sovereign ghostly pleasance in my soul. I was fulfilled with the everlasting sureness, mightily sustained without any painful dread. This feeling was so glad and so ghostly that I was in all peace and in rest, that there was nothing in earth that should have grieved me.

This lasted but a while, and I was turned and left to myself in heaviness, and weariness of my life, and irksomeness of myself, that scarcely I could have patience to live. There was no comfort nor none ease to me but faith, hope, and charity; and these I had in truth, but little in feeling.

This was being written in Norwich at precisely the same time that, two counties away, the *Pearl* was being put into form. The fact that such identity of spirit informed English prose and poetry of the same period, no less than the prose and poetry on the continent, is more important to the understanding of the fourteenth century literature and this particular bit of it, than that any one of these books might have been a source of the other.

Here, then, in the first sixty lines of the *Pearl,* is the picture of a desolate soul, deprived of heavenly consolation, he knows not why. While in a state of rebellious quest for it, he "slides" into sleep and is comforted wondrously by a dream that comes. This dream constitutes the body of the poem; it is followed by five stanzas in conclusion which show the poet awakened from his marvelous vision, his state of soul completely altered by all that he has heard and seen. He has spoken face to face with a real Pearl, manifested to him as a beautiful young girl, has learned from her the passing value of the pearl he mourned as lost, the abiding quality of the real Pearl, the rewards of heaven and the means of grace afforded him by which to attain these; he has been given St. John's glimpse into the third heaven of God's infinite glory. He is carried away with delight, would have rushed with the impetuosity of exalted desire (one is reminded here of St. Peter, and the "sons of thunder") immediately to the beatitude of his everlasting reward, but is withheld. He says:

> Delight so drove me, eye and ear;
> melted to madness my mortal mind;

when I saw my Precious, I would be there,
beyond the stream, though she were held.
Nothing, methought, might hinder me
from fetching birr and taking-off;
and nought should keep me from the start,
though I there perish'd swimming the rest.
But I was shaken from that thought;
as I wildly willed to start a-stream,
I was recalled from out that mood;
It was not pleasing to my Prince.

Here is a change of mood, indeed. The vision
of his Precious has so enthralled the poet that he
is ready to join her immediately or perish in the
impossible attempt. But all the wildness of his
desire subsides at the thought that this impetuosity might not please his Prince. Recall here
that just as he fell asleep, he would not be restrained even by Christ Himself. A transformation has been wrought; the wretched and disconsolate man who, a few hours before, had been
murmuring at the ways of God, is now restrained
even from too ardent a desire for heaven, knowing that such over-eagerness may perhaps grieve
his gracious Lord. It is literally a "conversion"
and is so called in spiritual parlance. Suso tells
of a like experience.

It happened once in the time of his beginnings, that
he came into the choir on St. Agnes' Day. . . . It was,

moreover, a time at which he was more than usually crushed down by a heavy weight of sorrow. Now it came to pass, that as he stood there all desolate, and with none to help or shield him, his soul was caught up in ecstasy, whether in the body or out of the body, and he saw and heard what no tongue can tell. It was without form or mode, and yet it contained within itself the entrancing delightfulness of all forms and modes. His heart was athirst and yet satisfied; his mind was joyous and blooming; wishes were stilled in him and desires had departed. He did but gaze fixedly on the dazzling effulgence in which he found oblivion of himself and all things. Was it day or night, he knew not. It was a breaking forth of the sweetness of eternal life, felt as present in the stillness of unvarying contemplation. This overpowering rapture lasted about an hour and a half; but whether his soul stayed in his body, or was parted from it, he knew not. When he came to himself again, he was altogether like a man who has come from another world. He came to himself with a deep groan, and his body sank to the ground, in spite of him, as if he were in a faint. He cried aloud piteously, and, deeply groaning, exclaimed: "Woe is me, my God! where was I? Where am I now?" Adding: "Ah, Thou, who art my heart's good! never can this hour pass from my heart!" This heavenly taste remained with him for a long time afterwards, and gave him a heavenly learning and longing after God.[76]

Humility, obedience, resignation are the inevitable consequences of such an experience as

---

[76] *The Life of Blessed Henry Suso*, by himself, London, pp. 9-11.

the poet has had; they are the result of Suso's revelation and of Juliana's "shewing." Ordinarily, such complete conversion is not the outcome of a nap, however poetic, in a graveyard, nor of a dream, however pleasant and consoling, of one's beloved dead.

The next stanza continues his act of complete detachment, the most desired and difficult of interior conquests.

> It pleased Him not I flung me thus,
> so madly, o'er those wondrous meres;
> though on I rush'd, full rash and rude,
> yet quickly was my running stay'd;
> for as I sped me to the brink,
> the strain me startled from my dream.
> Then woke I in that garden green;
> my head upon that mound was laid,
> e'en where my Pearl had strayed below.
> I roused me, and fell in great dismay,
> and, sighing, to myself I said,
> "Now, all be as that Prince may please!"

Suso speaks in his *Life* of the exceeding difficulty of attaining to this state of self-abnegation (p. 67).

He proceeded to hold converse with himself interiorly, saying: Look inwards, friend, and thou wilt find thyself still really there, and wilt perceive that, notwithstanding all thy outward practices, in which thou didst of thy own choice exercise thyself, thou art still undetached from self. . . . Thou art terrified every day at the sufferings which come upon thee. It may well be true that thou needest a higher school. Then sighing inwardly, he looked up to God, and said: "O God, how nakedly has this truth been shown me! Woe is me! When shall I ever become a truly detached man?"

The Blessed John Ruysbroeck puts this total self-immolation on the fourth step of *Love's Gradatory* (p. 71) in this beautiful figure:

After this flows the fourth stream of the humble life which is the total abandonment of all self-will and all that touches self. This stream takes its rise in suffering patiently endured. The humble, touched interiorly by the Spirit of God, perfected and transported into Him, renounces self and voluntarily abandons all to the care of God. He thus acquires one and the same will with the Divine Will, so that it is no longer possible nor lawful to desire and will anything but that which God wills.

One would think that the *Pearl* poet had this lesson, this model before him, so close is his imitation.

He rouses himself from his transport and sighing, says to himself:

Me pleased it ill to be out cast
so suddenly from that fair realm,
from all those sights so blithe and brave.
Sore longing struck me, and I swoon'd,
and ruefully then I cried aloud:
"O Pearl," quoth I, "of rich renown,
how dear to me was all that thou
in this true vision didst declare!

And if the tale be verily true,
that thou thus farest, in garland gay,
so well is me in this dungeon dire,
that thou art pleasing to that Prince!"

That Prince to please had I still bow'd,
nor yearn'd for more than was me given,
and held me there with true intent,
as the Pearl me pray'd, that was so wise,
belike, unto God's presence drawn,
to more of His mysteries had I been led.
But aye will man seize more of bliss
than may abide with him by right.
Wherefore my joy was sunder'd soon,
and I cast forth from realms eterne.
Lord, mad are they that 'gainst Thee strive,
or 'gainst Thy pleasure proffer aught.

To please the Prince, to be at peace,
good Christian hath it easy here;
for I have found Him, day and night,
A God, a Lord, a Friend full firm.
Over yon mound had I this hap,
prone there for pity of my Pearl;
To God I then committed it,
in Christ's dear blessing and mine own,—
Christ that in form of bread and wine
the priest each day to us doth shew;
He grant we be His servants leal,
yea, precious Pearls to please Him aye!

If, on the one hand, the poet is keenly sensitive
and responsive to his Prince's will, he is no less
conscious of his own. His conversion has not

made him an automaton—frankly, it pleased him
ill to be cast so suddenly out of his garden of
delights. But almost immediately the significance
of his experience strikes him. One thing is certain—it is well for him in the prison of this life
that his Pearl is pleasing to God. And another
conviction—if he had been perfectly selfless in
his resignation to that Prince, more bent on pleasing Him, as the Pearl had prayed him to be,
perhaps he would have been granted a more complete vision of God, fuller initiation into His
mysteries. Would this, I ask, have been his first
reaction, upon waking from a lovely dream of a
little daughter, or even a sweetheart? The
Orpheus-Eurydice situation, in its best Christian
versions, does not work out to this dénouement.
Silvius, in Boccaccio's *Olympia,* protests in true
paternal fashion, leaving no question of relationship or bereavement:

Quo tendis? quo, nata, fugis, miserumque parentem
Implicitum linquis lacrimis? Heu cessit in auras
Aethereas, traxitque simul, quos duxit, odores.
In mortem lacrimis ibo, ducamque senectam.[77]

---

[77] Whither, my daughter, whither fleest thou,
   leaving thy father tearful? Ah, she passed
   to upper air, and drew the scents she brought.
   With tears my life I'll dree, and fare to death.

Boccaccio's *Olympia,* edited, with modern rendering by Sir
Israel Gollancz in *Pearl,* London, 1921, p. 285.

But Ruysbroeck, out of his spiritual initiation, says:

> To die to sin is to live to God, to be emptied of self and detached from all that pleases or displeases, leads to the Kingdom of God; heart and desire must close to things of earth to open to God and things eternal, if we desire to taste and see that the Lord is sweet (*Love's Gradatory*, p. 124).

One sees at a glance to which of these the *Pearl* is kin. Additional evidence will make assurance doubly sure. Suso, in his *Book of Eternal Wisdom* (pp. 75, 76), tells of a vision of heaven granted him, and concludes in almost the words of the poet:

> The Servant: O wonder above all wonders! Ah, fathomless good, what art Thou? Yes, my gentle Lord, my chosen One, how good it is to be here! O my only Love, let us tarry here!
> Eternal Wisdom: It is not yet time to tarry here. Many a sharp conflict hast thou still to endure. This vision has only been shown to thee that thou mayest presently revert to it in all thy sufferings, as thou canst never lose courage, and wilt forget all thy sorrow; and further, as an answer to the complaint of foolish men who say that I allow My friends to fare so hard. See then what a difference there is between My friendship and the friendship of this temporal state; and to speak according to the truth, how much better than others My friends fare at My hands. My friends have bodily dis-

tress, but then they have peace of heart. The friends
of the world hunt after bodily comfort and ease, but
in their hearts, their souls and minds, they gain nothing
but trouble and vexation.

The Servant: Those persons, Lord, are out of their
right senses, and are raving, who would needs compare
Thy faithful friendship and the world's friendship together. O Lord, how very soft and gentle is Thy
Fatherly rod! Blessed is he on whom Thou sparest
it not. Lord, I now plainly see that tribulation does
not proceed from Thy harshness, but rather from Thy
tender love. Grant, O Lord, that these two visions
may never disappear from the eyes of my heart, so that
I never may lose Thy friendship.

Such identity of expression upon an unhack-
neyed theme must signify identity of spirit. The
spirit of Suso, and Ruysbroeck is unquestionably
mystical; it follows that *Pearl* belongs to their
household. The poet, indeed, blames himself for
every diminution of joy that he has suffered; it
is man's weakness to seize more bliss than is his
right, even as Suso says. And for this he is cast
forth from his realm of vision; from which he
very soberly concludes that they are mad who
strive against God's will or make the least protest
against His pleasure. One thinks of Angela of
Foligno and her piquant retort to God, who reminded her of her limitations in the realm of
vision. Critics have neglected these four stanzas

in their very important bearing on the body o
poem. Likewise they have slighted the last staꞮ
which is the crux of the entire *Pearl*.

The poem began on the discordant theme of the
poet's plaint, the Self motif; it ends on the beautiful harmony of peace, complete union of the
soul with its God, its Lord, its Friend. It is a
peace surpassing human understanding, begotten
of the abandonment of all that is dearest in life
to God; begotten more divinely through the
Blessed Sacrament which, under the appearance
of bread and wine, the poet beheld, perhaps received every morning at Mass. There is not the
remotest reference to death or bereavement here;
and in the concluding lines, where naturally the
poet would address his daughter if he had had
one, he identifies humanity, his friends, or religious
brethren with precious pearls. Plainly, he is not
mixing his figure. His uniform skill in keeping
his pattern of metaphor and allegory clear would
hardly have broken down in the last eight lines
in which he has all other matter under such sweet
and beautiful control. But here, with the tech-
nical instinct of a Poe, he goes straight back to
the opening stanza of the poem, to remind the
reader of all the circumstances of his rebellious
complaint, and then says: To God I have committed my Pearl; and through His grace we

shall all be His servants, yea, His precious pearls
—amen! Suppose for a moment that Pearl was
his baby daughter—with what an utter absurdity
the poem would conclude. Such a meaning,
though in spots through the poem it seems to
obtain, fails entirely here where, by all that is
consistent and artistic, it ought to have held. A
spiritual purification, a resignation of soul, a docility of spirit is what the poet has attained in
exchange for undue impetuosity, over-eagerness,
a greediness of soul. This is his final confession,
concluded by his steadfast hope of the ultimate
perfection and perseverance in this state through
the Blessed Sacrament. I know of no elegy that
even approaches this conclusion; I know of no
experience in spiritual desolation that does not
terminate so. The language of Ruysbroeck is certain:

I seem to be talking absurdly, but they who love will
understand me. Now the love of Jesus is of noble nature; where He has consumed He desires also to nourish.
. . . He makes the present of an eternal hunger and
thirst. In this hunger and thirst He gives His Body
and Blood for food. When we partake of them with
interior devotion, His Blood, full of warmth and glory,
flows from God into our veins. Love draws its object
forcibly unto itself; we draw Jesus into ourselves; Jesus
draws into Himself and there devours us. Then we
grow in stature; and carried above ourselves, above rea-

son into the interior of love, we devour spiritually. This immense love burns and consumes us and our spirit, and draws us into the unity where beatitude awaits us.[78]

Suso's attitude toward the Blessed Sacrament is indicated from this conversation recorded in almost the concluding chapter of the *Book of Eternal Wisdom* (pp. 137-139).

The Servant: But, Lord, if a man in his own opinion remains the same, and cannot prove that he either increases or decreases by it (the Blessed Sacrament) in holiness, or if he is often visited by spiritual dryness, how should he behave himself?

Eternal Wisdom: A man, provided only he does his part, should not withdraw himself because of spiritual dryness. For the salvation of that soul which, by God's will, suffers from spiritual dryness is often accomplished by the light of pure faith alone, as in great sweetness.

After which the servant breaks out into a prayer, preparatory for Holy Communion, which concludes:

Yes, Thou art the innocent Paschal Lamb, which at this day is still offered up for the sins of all mankind. . . . Enlighten my understanding with the light of true faith. Inflame my will with Thy sweet love. Cheer up my mind with Thy glad presence, and give virtue and perfection to all my powers. Watch over me at

---

[78] *Reflections from the Mirror of a Mystic,* translated from the Works of Ruysbroeck by Earle Baillie, London, 1905, pp. 76-80.

my death, that I may enjoy Thy beatific vision in eternal
bliss.

The most exacting critic could hardly ask for a
closer parallel to the poet's concluding aspiration.

The literature of the Blessed Sacrament repeats
and reinforces this parallelism. *The Revelations
of St. Gertrude,* Chapter xx, enumerates, again
just before the recapitulation of all her visions,
the six gifts that she has received through "the
supercœlestial banquet of Thy most sacred Body
and Blood." A comparatively unknown writer of
the first half of the thirteenth century, William
de Shoreham, Vicar of Chart, near Ledes, writes
thus beautifully of the Holy Eucharist in a poem
"De septem sacramentis," which in general content leans entirely to the side of dogma and away
from devotion:

> And yef mennes devocioun slaketh,
> Wonne he by-healdeth,
> For hyt thinkth bote other bread
> An-heagh that the prest healdeth;
> By-thenche hym
> Of the vertue that ther hys,
> That non errour adrenche hym.
>
> And tak ensaumple of that he kneuth,
> The preciouse stone,
> Thagh he hygge amange othere y-lyche,
> Me honoureth hym alone,

So swete;
Mid al thy wyl ther vertye hys,
God self ine sacrement y-mete.[79]

The poems of Shoreham are much less widely
known than *Pearl,* but there is a definiteness and
an orthodoxy of doctrine in all of them, indicative
of entire theological clearness upon the most difficult theological problems, the freedom of the will,
the foreknowledge of God, the dispensation of
grace through the sacramental system. Shoreham
was writing these intensely religious poems in
Kent a century before *Pearl,* another indication
of the pervasiveness of this spiritual impulse—
it was not, as has been said, a sporadic nor a local
outburst. No more is the place of climax and
emphasis which the *Pearl* poet gives to the Holy
Eucharist in his poem a matter of expediency or
accident. It was as native to his century as elec-
tricity is to our own. Life was bound up in it.

2. A Textual Study of the Dream Proper

It is in the light of these five introductory and
five concluding stanzas that the poem will be interpreted. What has happened to cause so complete a change, or, as the saints of those days

---

[79] *Poems of William de Shoreham,* edited by Thomas Wright,
London, 1849, p. 30.

would have termed it, "conversion"? The poet has enjoyed, as has been said, a vision of a radiant girl, clad in white and adorned with pearls. He has deliberately concealed the thing he has lost under the figure of a pearl, and to create a "pearl atmosphere" he says:

> And the gravel I ground upon that strand
> Were precious pearls of Orient. (ll. 81, 82)

Here is a difficulty. If the *Pearl* is to be identified with a dead daughter, this figure of grinding pearls upon the ground becomes a thing of crude and utter roughness. It would be as if the poet in the *Romaunt of the Rose* had dismantled all the garden of Love in his quest for the supreme bud, or as if the half-mad lover in *Maud* trampled and crushed all the roses in the dew-kissed garden on his way to the "Queen-Rose." However, if the poet had come into a state of spiritual enlightenment, the very ground on which his spirit trod would be composed of true interior joy. Juliana of Norwich sees in a vision a Servant before the Lord, in whom "inwardly . . . was showed a ground of love: which love that he had to the Lord was ever-like to the love that the Lord had to him" (p. 114—a figure which she repeats often, pp. 135-137). One can well imagine that sunbeams would be "but dim and dark" against such a glory, but the radiance of ground pearls is a questionable thing!

In the magic wonder of the place the poet forgot all grief, which would be highly improbable in the case of an inconsolable father. Such beauty would be to him rather a mockery than a source of complete oblivion. I quote the stanzas and beside them the vision of the Cœlum Empyreum vouchsafed to Henry Suso by Eternal Wisdom (p. 71).

Wondrously the hill-sides shone
with crystal cliffs that were so clear;
and all about were holt-woods bright,
with boles as blue as hue of Inde;
and close-set leaves on every branch
as burnish'd silver sway'd and swung;
when glided 'gainst them glinting gleams,
splendent they shone with shimmering sheen;
and the gravel I ground upon that strand
were precious pearls of Orient;
the sunbeams were but dim and dark,
if set beside that wondrous glow!

'Mid the magic of those wondrous hills
my spirit soon forgot all grief;
flavors of fruit so fresh were there,
as food full well they gave me strength;
birds in the wood together flew,
of flaming hues, both small and great;
nor citrole string nor citherner
could e'er re-tell their goodly glee;

for when those birds did beat their wings
they sang with such a sweet accord
no rapture could so stir a man
as to hear and see that wonderment.

All was so dight in wondrous wise,
no tongue of man hath power to tell
the beauty of that forest-land,
where fortune led me on and on.
Still forth I pressed in blissful mood;
no hill, though high, might hinder me.
Deeper in wood, more fair arose
plains and plants and spice and fruits,
hedgerows and borders and river-meads;
as fine gold-thread were their steep banks.
A water I reach'd that cleft the strand,—
Lord, how wondrous was the sight!   (ll. 73-108)

The Servant: O Lord, through Thy goodness, dare I hope that Thou wilt tell me yet more about my fatherland, so that I may long for it all the more, and may suffer every affliction the more cheerfully? . . .

Eternal Wisdom: Now, then, ascend thou on high with Me. I will carry thee thither in spirit, and will give thee, after a rude similitude a distant glimpse into the future. See how the delightful city shines with beaten gold, how it glitters with costly jewels, inlaid with precious stones, transparent as crystal, reflecting red roses, white lilies, and all living flowers. Now, look on the beautiful heavenly fields themselves, Lo! here all delights of summer, here sunny meads of May, here the very valley of bliss, here the glad moments are seen flitting from joy to joy; here harps and viols, here

singing and leaping, and dancing, hand in hand forever!
here the gratification of every desire, here pleasure without pain and everlasting security!

Comment on the similarity of the passages is
superfluous; it may be useful to remark again that
the poet, on his anonymous quest, is experiencing
delights and revelations identical with those
granted to mystics in their progress toward perfect detachment and interior peace, and is under-
going none of the conditions normal to the sorrows of bereavement. Hence the obvious conclusion; his is a spiritual quest, of which his poem
is the chronicle.

His desolation is completely forgotten in his
eagerness to press on to new marvels in this won-
derland. Hills do not hinder him, but he cannot
so easily overcome the barrier of "a water,"
devised, he says, like a moat, beyond which lay
the bounds of a fair castle. The water is so deep
that he dares not wade; and he cannot find a ford
for all that he "stalked along the bank." This
activity and manifest interest and pleasure in his
new situation is, I say, the very reverse of what
a bereaved parent would feel or display in the
same situation, much less deliberately perpetuate
in poetry. The pool, the poet remarks, was set
with jewels; each pebble was an emerald, a sap-
phire, or a goodly gem, quite as Suso saw them.

And as he looks across "that merry mere," he sees a child sitting, "a maid of grace," in "glistening white"—he knows her, for he has seen her before. He gazes steadfastly at her, and the longer he looks, he knows her "more and more." There is a sense of growing penetration, of gradually perfected perception in this not at all consistent with the recognition of a person. If this were his child, he would have recognized her, not only at once, but completely, in the brightness of a place that made the very pebbles at the bottom of the river plainly visible. Moreover, he would have been precipitate in reaching her as he was in crossing the very stream for no other reason than reaching the beauties beyond. Instead he says: "Long toward her there I look'd." This is a process of authentic contemplation such as has already been quoted from the *Life of Suso*. The fruits are such as the contemplative knows and holds precious:

> The more I scann'd her face so fair,
>
> .   .   .   .   .   .
>
> Such gladdening glory came to me
> As seldom had been wont to come.

The poet wishes to address his vision, but wonder restrains him, surprise at finding her in so strange a place. Now, not even the most ortho-

dox exponent of infant baptism would be shocked
to find an unbaptized child in this earthly Paradise. The Limbo of the unbaptized is a place of
surpassing loveliness, and lacks only the vision of
God to make it heaven. A man so thoroughly
instructed in doctrine as the poet would never have
betrayed such ignorance of dogma about the condition of children after death. But if this is a
state of his own soul, the situation changes. Theo-
logians hold that the beauty of a human soul is
so great as almost to overpower one who should
behold it in this life. And if a virtuous person
could contemplate his own soul, he would be
equally amazed. In like manner, if he could behold his sufferings as God sees them, he would
be bewildered at their transfiguration. Hagiography bristles with proof of this. The sixteenth
Revelation of Juliana of Norwich is only one (pp.
167, 168):

And then our Lord opened my spiritual eye and
shewed me my soul in midst of my heart. I saw the
Soul so large as it were an endless world, and as it
were a blissful kingdom, and by the conditions that I
saw therein I understood that it is a worshipful City.
In the midst of the City sitteth our Lord Jesus, God
and Man. . . . And in this [sight] He shewed the sat-
isfying that He hath of the making of Man's Soul.
For as well as the Father might make a creature, and
as well as the Son could make a creature, so well would

the Holy Ghost that Man's Soul were made; and so it was done. And therefore the blessed Trinity enjoyeth without end in making of Man's Soul: for he saw from without beginning what should please Him without end. . . . And thus I understood in verity that our Soul may never have rest in things that are beneath itself. And when it cometh above all creatures into the Self, yet it may not abide in the beholding of its Self, but all the beholding is blissfully set in God that is the Maker dwelling therein. For in Man's Soul is His very dwelling; and the highest light and the brightest shining of the City is the glorious love of our Lord, as to my sight.

This is the beginning of the poet's supernatural intercourse with his own soul. He is speaking, indeed, to a dream-child, but this child is not the ghost of a dead infant. It is the personification of his own soul in the state of such potential perfection and happiness as is congruous to it at this time of his life. The Pearl is symbolic of this same state and is used interchangeably with the Maiden or Child to indicate it. That such inter-relation is possible one has on this evidence, or from this word of Angela of Foligno:

And I saw myself in two divisions . . . and in one division I saw love and every good which was God's and not mine, and in the other I saw myself, dry, and I saw I had nothing good belonging to me.[80]

---

[80] *Catholic Mysticism,* Algar Thorold, London, 1900, p. 147.

The poet's condition, precisely. The discrepancy between these two divisions fills him with dread, especially as the "spotless child of grace" arises in all her royal array to speak to him. The detail mentioned here, "she was nearer to me than aunt or niece, wherefore my joy was much the more," does not at all force the alternative that she must have been a daughter. There are a number of relationships, physical or spiritual, nearer than those suggested. A man ingenious enough to write *Pearl* would hardly have concealed a daughter under such a ruse. The lines I take to indicate a nearness outside of and beyond kinship of nature. If the poet was a religious as so much of the poem indicates, he would have no nearer female relative as a basis for comparison.

This vision offers speech to the poet, in womanly fashion, "in womanly lore," another impossibility for an infant of two years; the content we are not told, only his reply. "O Pearl," he asks, "art thou my pearl, that I have plain'd—so lone, a-night?" and presses his question further. He knows not how she has reached this "life of Joy," while he in "dolorous plight" is cast. The jewel puts on her crown and answers gravely:

> Sir, thou hast misread thy tale,
> to say thy pearl is all perdu. (ll. 257, 258)

and assures him that his treasure is safe where
no mourning or loss can ever touch it. Then she
adds most significantly:

> if thou must lose
> thy joy for a gem that to thee was dear,
> thou'rt set, methinks, on mad intent,
>
> what thou didst lose was but a rose,
> that flower'd and fail'd, as Nature bade. (ll. 265-270)

This is precisely what every spiritual director
tells persons lamenting a subtraction of spiritual
consolation; their loss is but the withering flower
of sensible devotion which does not at all affect
the root of their devotion. Indeed, they are frequently laughed at for mistaking for true goodness an emotion or a feeling of piety, and their
mistake is ordinarily regarded as an evidence of
their youth in religion. Cassian says in his second
Conference, Chapter x:

> It [the pious formula, "O God, make speed to help
> me"] warns us whose lot is spiritual success and de-
> light of heart that we ought not to be at all elated or
> puffed up by our happy condition, which it assures us
> cannot last without God as our protector.

And Thomas à Kempis, the poet's great contemporary, wrote out of his intimate experience:

I never found any one so religious and devout, as not to have sometimes a subtraction of grace, or feel a diminution of fervor. . . . For temptation going before is usually a sign of ensuing consolation. For heavenly comfort is promised to such as have been proved by temptations (*Imitation*, II. 9).

The danger of emotional devotion is one of the first things against which a young religious must be guarded. It is the food from which, in his spiritual infancy, he must be weaned. The deprivation is to him as dismaying as it is necessary. Again, Thomas à Kempis says:

For who is there . . . that would not willingly receive comfort and spiritual joy, if he could always have it. . . . He that has been taught by the gift of grace, and instructed by the scourge of the withdrawing of it, will not dare to attribute anything good to himself (*Imitation*, II. 10).

These are my preliminary reasons for thinking that the *Pearl* poet was himself a religious, or at least was portraying the spiritual adventures of a young religious. He has no doubt, after the maiden's reproof, that the pearl which he lamented was a perishable thing, and through a series of puns on *jewels* and *pearls,* he rejoices in the recovery of the real jewel of his quest:

A jewel to me was then this guest,
and jewels were her gentle words.

"Indeed," quoth I, "Bless'd dearest mine
My dire distress away thou draw'st.
I make request to be excused;
I trowe'd my Pearl had pass'd from Day;
but now 'tis found, I shall make mirth,
and dwell with it in radiant groves,
and praise my Lord and all His laws,
who hath me brought this bliss anigh.
Were I with thee beyond these waves,
I were a joyful jeweler!" (ll. 277-288)

The text leaves no doubt as to the two pearls, the one sought and the one found; it makes equally clear the poet's illumination as to his mistake, and his joy in his great consolation.

One comes now to a closer study of the dialogue between the child and the poet (she never calls herself the *Pearl*). She tells him that he was set on mad intent, if he lost his joy for a gem, "which through the casket's case enclosing it . . . now is proved a pearl of price." One stops at these lines which are quite incapable of application to a child. Certainly the beauty and joy of the vision is in no way due to a decomposing body in a supposed grave; and yet the figurative meaning of casket must be the body of the child if one reads the poem as an elegy. Merit, the reward of heaven both in degree and kind, depends on the manner in which one has lived in the flesh. Thus, the body is the casket containing the soul, and virtues practiced through it prove to be pearls of price to every individual in eternity. This meaning is emphatic in the last four lines of the stanza:

> And thou hast call'd thy fate a thief,
> that ought from nought hath made for thee;
> thou blamest the balm of all thine ill,
> thou art a graceless jeweler. (ll. 273-276)

In other words, your cross, or desolation which has made active virtue of what was before nothing, nonexistence, this trial is really a boon, a blessing to you, but you blame it, graceless jeweler!

Eternal Wisdom says to Henry Suso (pp. 77-79):

> What I mean is every kind of suffering, whether willingly or unwillingly accepted or unwillingly incurred as when a man makes a virtue of necessity in not wishing to be exempt from suffering without My will and ordering it, in humble patience, to My eternal praise; and the more willingly he does this, the more precious and agreeable it is to Me. . . . Such is My eternal order in all nature, from which I do not swerve; what is precious and good must be earned with bitterness; he who recoils at this, let him recoil; many are indeed called but few are chosen.
>
> Conform thyself freely to My will under every pain which I ordain thee to suffer, without excepting this or the other suffering. Dost thou not know that I only desire what is best for thee, even with as kindly a feel-

ing as thou myself? Hence it is that I am Eternal Wisdom, and that I know better than thou what is for thy good.

Hadst thou so much spiritual sweetness and divine consolation and heavenly delight as, at all times, to overflow with the divine dew, it would not be for thee so very meritorious of itself, since, for all this together, I should not have to thank thee so much.

Juliana's version of this state is as quaintly beautiful as all her other utterances. She says (pp. 24, 25):

And thus was I learned, to mine understanding, that seeking is as good as beholding, for the time that He will suffer the soul to be in travail. It is God's will that we seek Him, to the beholding of Him, for by that He shall shew us Himself . . . when He will. . . . It is God's Will that we have three things in our seeking: The first is that we seek earnestly and diligently, without sloth, and, as it may be, through His grace, without unreasonable heaviness and vain sorrow. The second is, that we abide Him steadfastly for His love without murmuring and striving against Him, till our life's end: for it shall last but a while. The third is that we trust in Him mightily of full assured faith. For it is His Will that we know that He shall appear suddenly and blissful to all that love Him.

One could search the lives of the saints from Saint Anthony of the Desert to St. Gabriel of the Passion or St. Joan of Arc, our two recently canonized, and find without exception the same lesson of suffering taught and learned.

The poet cannot but be consoled—and here he says his Pearl is found which he thought had passed from day. Even vision would not change the fact of death, and possession would be but a fleeting thing; the poet here expresses complete restoration of what he has lost and anticipation of future enjoyment of it. "I shall make mirth and dwell with it in radiant groves, and praise my Lord in all His laws." (ll. 283, 284.) His happiness is not contingent nor conditional. And as a reflection he sighs, "Were I with thee beyond these waves I were a joyful jeweller!" (ll. 287, 288)—that is, were my condition confirmed by death, I should, indeed, be joyful; however, I shall dwell in contentment with the true consolation of God and bless Him for bringing "this bliss nigh." It is the spirit of à Kempis, which says, "To Thee I lift up mine eyes; in Thee, O my God, the Father of mercies I put my trust. Bless and sanctify my soul with Thy heavenly blessing, that it may be made Thy holy habitation and the seat of Thy eternal glory; and let nothing be found in the temple of Thy dignity that may offend the eyes of Thy majesty" (*Imitation*, III. 59).

Another essential point here; what the poet is

evidently seeking and finding is not comfort in
bereavement or solace in loss, but a very personal
consolation for an acutely spiritual and interior
affliction. There is not a suggested desire for
the continued earthly existence of another person,
nor an expressed anticipation of the joy of reunion with one distinct from the writer; the thing
he mourns has gone from his own soul; the thing
he receives enters his soul; and its continued
possession he anticipates in himself, which makes
it exceedingly difficult to regard Pearl as a person.
It becomes almost impossible, in the presence of
such accumulating evidence of spiritual autobiography, to read an elegiac meaning into the
poem.

At this point the maiden turns theologian and
from her discourse, one gets no uncertain notion
of the philosophical basis on which the poem rests.
The author was a true Scholastic with every well
developed feeling for classification, enumeration,
argument, and proof. "Jeweler," says the gem,
"why jest ye men—so mad ye are!"   (ll. 289,
290). The case of the poet is not isolated, evidently; "ye men" have mistook God's ways repeatedly; she is correcting a general fault. No
trimmer is the Maiden, no modern positivist, no
rationalist. She will not make God a liar, Who
promises resurrection though He inflicts death

in the flesh. And here, in line 306, is the first
mention of death in the poem, entirely without
elegiac suggestion.

> I hold that jeweler little to praise
>
> .   .   .   .   .   .
>
> that thinketh our Lord would speak a lie,
> who leally promised to raise thy life,
> though fortune gave thy flesh to death.

It is the Maiden who speaks; it is to the death
of any individual that she refers, not to an experience which has touched either herself or the
poet. If the poem is one of mourning for a
child, this is the opportunity for some word of
consolation, some promise of reunion. There is
none; death is mentioned with an utter remote-
ness to the theme of the poem. Flatly the maiden
says it is an overweening thing which ill befits
a righteous man to trust nothing save what his
"mere reason" tells him. And without more ado,
she administers what I call her threefold scold-
ing; she reprimands the poet for three things
specifically and then explains his error in each of
them. First, he believes that she is in this vale
because he sees her there with his eyes; second,
he wishes to remain there with her; third, he
wishes to cross the river that separates him from
her. All this is wrong, and she tells him why.

You have read Christ's word all wrong, if you
trust only what you see with your eyes, she says
in substance. What other avenues of faith are
there except faith and intuition? And these are
the chosen sources of the mystic's knowledge.
Even the great rationalist, Thomas Aquinas, put
aside his last work incomplete because he said
he had seen in union with God, things that made
all his reasoning seem slight and poor. It is
difficult to choose or to limit quotation here, so
completely do faith and intuitive knowledge per-
meate all mystical writing, from St. Paul's
"whether in the body or out of the body, I know
not" through St. Teresa's *Interior Castle*, St.
John of the Cross' *Dark Night of the Soul*, Dom
Savinien Louismet's *Mystical Initiation*. Suso,
Tauler, Ruysbroeck, Richard Rolle, Juliana of
Norwich are the most authentic exponents of this
mystical knowledge in the poet's own century.

Juliana has a very neat statement of this plight
of the poet, as well as the solution offered by the
Maiden:

This saw I bodily, troublously and darkly; and I desired more bodily sight, to have seen more clearly. And
I was answered in my reason: *If God will shew thee
more, He shall be thy light: thee needeth none but Him.*
For I saw Him sought.

For we are now so blind and unwise that we never

seek God till He of His goodness shew Himself to us. And then we ought to see of Him graciously, then are we stirred by the same grace to seek with great desire to see Him more blissfully.

And thus I saw Him, and sought Him, and I had Him, I wanted Him (p. 22).

And after this I saw God in a Point, that is to say, in mine understanding (p. 26).

And after this, ere God shewed any words, He suffered me for a convenient time to give heed unto Him, and all that I had seen, and all intellect that was therein, as the simplicity of the soul might take it.

Then He, without voice and opening of lips, formed in my soul these words (p. 30).

This is the mystic's theory of knowledge exemplified; knowledge so acquired was, according to the Maiden, to be trusted at least as much as that acquired by reason. Suso's entire spiritual life was led under direct guidance of Eternal Wisdom; the translator's preface to his *Life* (xxxi) says that when he was about to be promoted to the degree of doctor in theology, "he was forbidden to accept this honour by a voice from God within him saying:—Thou knowest well enough already how to give thyself to God and to draw other men to Him by thy preaching." His entire *Book of Eternal Wisdom* he himself says is the outcome of "many a bright inspiration of divine truth." This intercourse between himself and Eternal Wis-

dom, he says, "took place not by bodily intercourse nor by figurative answers; it took place
solely by meditation in the light of Holy Writ
whose answers can deceive in nothing" (p. 21).
Again, in his *Life,* he describes such a revelation
of the condition of his soul as very closely re-
sembles the poet's:

It came to pass once, after the time of his suffering
was over, that early one morning he was surrounded
in a vision by the heavenly spirits. Whereupon he be-
sought one of the bright princes of heaven to show him
the manner of God's secret dwelling in his soul. The
Angel answered thus:—Cast, then, a joyous glance into
thyself, and see how God plays His play of love with thy
loving soul. He looked immediately, and saw that his
body over his heart was clear as crystal, and that in
the center of his heart was sitting tranquilly, in loving
form, the Eternal Wisdom; beside whom there sat, full
of heavenly longing, the Servitor's (Suso's) soul, which,
leaning lovingly towards God's side, and encircled by
God's arms, and pressed close to His divine heart, lay
thus entranced and drowned in love in the arms of the
beloved God (pp. 21, 22).

Thomas à Kempis implies the same distrust
of sense-knowledge and reliance on revelation in:

Our opinion and our sense often deceive us and dis-
cover but little; happy is he whom Truth teacheth by
itself, not by figures and words that pass, but as it is
in itself (*Imitation,* I.3).

All of this implied discussion would have very little relevance to an elegy, but it is knit up into the very essence of mystical autobiography, and is particularly important in this one. Because the very effectiveness of the poet's vision depends on his faith in it; his was a plight in which his disappointed feelings had reduced him to despair; spiritual healing must come to him from some source beyond reason. This vision was granted to him precisely to reëstablish his faith in conditions that he could not see with his physical eyes, but for proofs of which he was pining. He was lamenting the state of his soul; he could not see that state and what he could feel of it led him almost to despair. He was sensible of no great virtue in it because he experienced no feelings of piety. His ideas of soul conditions were badly tangled with his sense perceptions. So, in a vision he is allowed to see just what his soul looks like, in the state which he so ardently desires, and of which he wishes some sensible proof. But at the same time, he is reproved for not trusting to the assurances of faith, at least as much as to the witness of his eyes, in the matter of its well-being. The situation is dramatic. His soul, the Maiden, says to him in substance: Here I am if you must see me—but why should your eyes convince you of my state more than your faith. Now that

you have seen me, be satisfied to trust of my condition, when, invisible to you, it is in God's keeping.

The Maiden is unmerciful in her second complaint. You say, she accuses, that you "will dwell
in this burgh; 'twere meet, methinks, first to ask
leave; and yet thou mightest miss the boon" (ll.
314-316). Were importunate pinions of desire
ever clipped with greater neatness and dispatch?
It would have delighted the soul of Teresa of
Avila, two centuries later, to have read that
stanza. And Thomas à Kempis says of this pre-
sumption:

> Some wanting discretion, have ruined themselves upon
> the occasion of the grace of devotion. . . . They become
> needy and were left in a wretched condition, who had
> built themselves a nest in heaven; to the end, that being
> thus humbled and impoverished, they might learn not
> to trust to their own wings, but to hide themselves
> under mine (*Imitation,* III. 7).

Again one wonders why a child should reprove
her lonely father for even a presumptuous desire
of heaven with her, or should express a doubt
about his achieving it at all.

The poet's third offense is treated with somewhat less severity. He wished to cross this stream
and so attain unchanging happiness. Such immediate transition has been made impossible by our

first parents, the Maiden tells him, so the cheer-less "goal" of death is now an intermediate experience through which man must pass. Here again death is mentioned but with no reference at all to the object of the poet's melancholy state. This is most strange if his loss is a bereavement. Living under the sentence of life, waiting for the release of death is a characteristic mystical attitude. Juliana says in her *Revelations* (pp. 220, 221).

And at the end of woe, suddenly our eyes shall be opened, and in clearness of light our sight shall be full: which light is God, our Maker and Holy Ghost, in Christ our Savior.

Henry Suso, after his vision of heaven, puts precisely the same request to Eternal Wisdom as does the poet to his vision.

The Servant:—Gentle Lord, my chosen One, how good it is to be here! O my only Love, let us tarry here!
Eternal Wisdom:—It is not yet time to tarry here. Many a sharp conflict hast thou still to endure. The vision has only been shown to thee that thou mayest presently revert to it in all thy sufferings, as thus thou canst never lose courage, and wilt forget all thy sorrow (p. 75).

The poet protests, human-wise—he almost pouts and does not care what happens to him, if he must again forego the lost joy that he has just recovered. He is indeed young in the ways of tribulation and knows only in theory the doctrine of Divine Love. "I am accustomed to visit my elect in two manners of ways, that is, by trials and by comfort," one reads in the *Imitation* (III, 3). His preceptress is patient with the poet; he thinks pessimistically of nought but grief, she says, on account of a few small losses; "many a man oft loseth more," or as à Kempis says: "What thou sufferest is but little, in comparison of them who have suffered so much. . . . The true patient man . . . takes it all with equality of mind, as from the hand of God, and esteems it a great gain" (*Imitation,* III. 19). And in the same chapter, "To suffer and to be afflicted . . . is very healthful for the soul." All of which is the very meat and marrow of spiritual counsel but not the tradition of elegiac poetry.

Here, in stanza xxx, the Maiden becomes dictatorial. "Doom thou the Lord," she says, "He will not swerve a foot from the way." Complaints are useless, cease to chide, better try humility, resignation; "thy prayer may His pity touch . . . His mercy . . . and His solace may assuage thy grief"; the counsel expressed already in a number of quotations. And again one is conscious that these counsels are directed to a state of soul. Prayers for a dead child are useless, in the sense of bettering its condition. The poet is to seek God's grace and mercy; certainly not for his innocent child. It must be for himself. The Vision holds out the hope that God's solace will so assuage his grief that *"all his losses"* will "glance lightly off." The death of a child would be but one loss; but in spiritual dryness one experiences a multitude of losses, sweetness, consolation, pleasure in prayer, joy in God's service, relish for spiritual things, sometimes even the hope of heaven. This justifies the implication of many sorrows.

The effect on the poet is magical; his perversity and childish pique have exhausted themselves and he is now ready for docility. "Let not my Lord be wroth with me," he exclaims, "if wildly I rave, rushing in speech—my heart with mourning all was torn." One looks back in thought to Cassian's description of the effects of spiritual dryness—"it makes it (the soul) impatient and rough in all its duties of work and devotion," and forward to St. Teresa's "I could eat people up," while in that state (*Autobiography*, p. 222), and realizes the identity of symptoms of a very common disease. That is the point. The talk in the *Pearl* is always of a spiritual disease and a way of being rid of it, by patience, humility, abandonment to the will of God. This preoccupation with maladies of soul, with the utter emptying oneself of one's own will, with acquiring the grace of God does not enter characteristically into elegiac reflection. It is part of the spiritual history of every religious; it is recorded in every spiritual autobiography and every authoritative book on the spiritual life; it is the conspicuous theme of *Pearl*.

The poet's speech of submission which follows, contains what has been regularly taken as an indication that Pearl was a child. He says:

> I wist not where my Pearl was gone.
> Now I it see, now less'neth my loss;
> and when we parted, at one we were;
> God forbid we be now wroth!
> We meet so seldom by stock or stone.

Supposing that the Pearl was a child, would any father, even in the wide fields of figurative poetry, have sought her at the tender age of two years, "by stock or stone"? The idea is incongruous. Also, is an infant capable of anything except acquiescence with its parents? "At one we were" loses all serious sense in such an interpretation. Besides, though the poet apparently has had no previous vision, such as he records here, he has met the Pearl, if only seldom, in the immediate past. This straightforward statement can hardly be explained as relating to a dead child—"we meet so seldom by stock or stone." But if it refers to spiritual consolation, it is not only consistent with, but proper to that condition, as abundant citations have shown. The speech I take as a simple and outspoken apology for the poet's rather rude complaint, a naïve explanation that, as he has lately enjoyed so seldom the happiness of spiritual joy, his lack of courtesy in receiving it is his misfortune rather than his fault. And he has Cassian and St. Teresa and many others for company. The religious who has waited long for consolation and then feels the happiness that the poet has described spontaneously makes many such confused acts of contrition for his impatience. But if he is apologizing to a baby, the thing becomes ridiculous. Ramon Lull says:

The trials and tribulations that the Lover endured for love's sake made him weary and apt to be impatient; and the Beloved reproved him, saying that he whom either trouble or happiness affected thus knew but little of love. So the Lover was contrite and wept, and he begged his Beloved to restore his love again (p. 92).

There was great strife and contention between Love and the Lover, because the Lover was incensed at the trials which Love made him to bear. And they debated whether Love or the Lover was to blame. So both of them came to the judgment-seat of the Beloved; and

He chastened the Lover with griefs and rewarded him
with increase of love (p. 76).

After this apology, the poet asks what manner
of life the Maiden of his vision lives. He gives
his reasons for asking; he is "a man with mourning marred"; but her estate, "so changed to worth
and weal," is "the high-way" of all his joy. She
answers happily, being most pleased with his
change of attitude. Now is he "welcome here to
bide and walk"; spiritual joy abides in humility,
but "masterful mood and mighty pride" are hated
in the life of spiritual perfection. She gives him
this exquisite cue:

My Master loveth not to blame,
.   .   .   .   .   .
And when in His place appear thou must,
in humbleness be deep devout.

There is no question of the Maiden's interest in
the poet; she is merciless with him when need be,
but so solicitously tender here. She tells him then
of the heaven of her condition and his ultimate
desire. She explains to him that she is the Bride
of the Lamb of God, as are also her companions.
Now there is only one class of persons on earth
who anticipate such an eternity; they are religious.

All religious think of heaven in exactly these terms; they are to be Brides of the spotless Lamb Whom virgins alone can approach. Theirs is to be no monotonous Shavian heaven spent in singing Alleluias between yawns, but the intensest and most spiritual of nuptial relations with Christ, their Lover. The *Ancren Riwle*, literal, didactic, and unemotional as it is, says:

> The love which Jesus Christ hath to his dear spouse surpasseth them all four [*i.e.*, love of friends of man and wife, of parent and child, of body and soul] and excelleth them all. . . . And therefore Christ loveth more; for though the soul, his spouse, should be unfaithful to him with the fiend of hell . . . his mercy is ever ready for her, whensoever she will come to him.

This is distinctly the reward neither of baptized infants nor of persons in the married state. Virginity is no virtue to them and its peculiar heaven would not constitute their perfect happiness. Does a two-year-old child, a radiantly beautiful girl, or a married man, however young and poetic, anticipate or hope to realize this beatific condition? Yet every religious does. Has any religious teacher ever taught the secular world to expect such a heaven? Yet that is the vision which sent St. Agnes to martyrdom and St. Francis to his bride of snow, that has given meaning to the vow of chastity for twenty centuries. It is the motif of the early English *Juliana* and the later *St. Katherine.* One meets it in the life of every virgin martyr. Clearly, I, as a religious, might depict for a person such an anticipation of my hoped-for heaven as the Pearl gives to the poet; but he, unless bound also by the vow of chastity, would not clamor almost rudely to join me in it. Unless the poet was a religious, the revelation falls flat; it is quite without point.

Here a significant thing happens. The Maiden says: "My Lord, the Lamb, took me in marriage—crowned me queen." The poet, with the intrepidity of great love, challenges her title. Mary, the Mother of God, is heaven's Queen; he will not bide an intruder, even if it be his own supreme bliss. It is quite unthinkable; he feels that it is an insult to Christian doctrine; he shows that it is an outrage to Mediæval devotion; "Art thou the Queen of heaven blue," he asks with recently acquired deference; "we believe in Mary . . . and who can take from her the crown?" (l. 424). If the humility of the poet has pleased the Maiden, his loyalty to Mary crowns her joy. She veils her face and kneeling, salutes her Lady; "Courteous Queen . . . matchless Mother, Merriest Maid, blest Beginner of every grace!" The tableau is beyond all passages in the poem exquisite and delicate, a breathing bit of Fra Angelico. Her obeisance over, the Maiden rises and addresses the poet doctrinally. The immediateness of this deferential gesture of his mind and soul toward the Blessed Virgin is typical of Catholics always and of religious and mystical-minded Catholics especially. Moreover, devotion to Mary was the great spiritual preoccupation of the Middle Ages. The love of Mary, the joys of Mary, the sorrows of Mary, the name of Mary were the themes of unnumbered lyrics; the help and protection of the Mother of God were the themes of a whole body of *exempla* and *contes devots*. These facts would justify this glorification of the Blessed Virgin in *Pearl*, perhaps, though such glorification would have no essential place in an elegy.

But if the poem is regarded as a spiritual autobiography, the situation changes completely. An exposition on our Lady is part of the technique of mediæval spiritual autobiography. Not a single important work of this type lacks it. One finds it in the *Ancren Riwle;* one chapter in the first part is devoted to the invocation and worship (used not in the absolute sense) of the Blessed Virgin, her joys, an extract of which reads:

Sweet Lady, Saint Mary, for the great joy that filled all the earth, when thy sweet blissful Son, received thee into his infinite bliss, and with his blissful arms placed thee on the throne, and a queenly crown on thy head brighter than the sun; O high, heavenly queen, so receive these salutations from me on earth, that I may blissfully salute thee in heaven.

Angela of Foligno records greater faith through the Blessed Virgin as the seventeenth step in her spiritual ascent (*Op. cit.*, p. 104); the eleventh Revelation of Juliana of Norwich, Chapter xxv, is a gracious introduction of the Mother to the lovers of her Son. "Wilt thou see her?" Christ asks, "I wot well that thou wilt see My Blessed Mother, for after myself she is the highest joy that I might show thee . . . and most she is desired to be seen of all my blessed creatures" (p. 3). It is not less gracious than Suso's presentation of the same lovely Lady in the *Book of Eternal Wisdom*, "Steal a little nearer," says Eternal Wisdom in showing to the Servant the joys of heaven, "and mark how the sweet queen of the celestial kingdom, whom thou lovest with so much ardour, soars aloft in dignity and joy over the whole celestial host, reclining tenderly on her beloved, encircled with rose-flowers and lilies of the valley. See how her ravishing beauty fills with delight and wonder all the heavenly choirs" (p.

71). In *Love's Gradatory* (p. 93) Ruysbroeck regards love of the Blessed Virgin one of the three ways of honoring God. Sermons 21, 22, 23, 24, 25 in the third part of Thomas à Kempis' *Sermons to the Novice Regular* are devoted to the veneration, praise, service, sorrow and joy, merits and privileges of Mary. In the very first pages of the *Fire of Love* Richard Rolle promises to the lovers of God incredible joy in "the blist maydin"; his Meditation on the Psalter of Mary is an expression of that joy experienced. "A talking of the love of God," [81] one of the most precious bits of anonymous Middle English writing of Rolle's school, begins its characteristic chapter on our Lady with this sweet invocation: "A milde Marie, moder of Merci, socour of serweful and comfort of care." Such devotional outpouring was not only a habit of sanctity fostered by a Bernard, a Bonaventure, a Dominic; it was as much a part and a tradition of spiritual expository writing as was the chapter on temptations or on miracles an essential of all hagiography. Thus, eulogy on our Lady in the *Pearl,* in no way typical of elegiac poetry, gives the poem another claim to a place among spiritual autobiographies.

By conscientious adherence to the text, we have

---

[81] C. Horstman, *Richard Rolle of Hampole,* London, 1896, Vol. II, pp. 123-128; pp. 346-366.

come to the passage which has been taken as conclusive proof that Pearl was the poet's infant daughter. The poet feels that the dignity of the Maiden in heaven is out of keeping with her youth. She herself has said, "of tender age, full young, was I" (ll. 412) and now the poet remonstrates with her:

> thou livedst not two years in our land,
> God thou couldst not please or pray,
> and never knewest Pater nor Creed!

from which it has been generally concluded that the Maiden addressed must be a child of two years old. That would be the natural, almost the only interpretation possible to the secular reader. But here the spiritual explanation fits best of all. It has almost the force of a literary *coup d'état*. For in religious life, one's age is counted by the number of years one has lived in his community, and not by natural age. For instance, a person of twenty-five enters a community. At thirty-five he is just ten years old in his order. Persons are referred to as young or old religious entirely according to their age in their order. Cassian says in his *Institutes,* Book IV, chapter 30:

A famous Abbot Pinufius left his monastery of which he was superior and out of love of subjection sought a distant monastery where he could be received as a novice. . . . Here they gave him the care of the garden. . . . And this he performed under another and a younger brother. . . . He was looked upon as the lowest of all, as being a novice and one who had but lately forsaken the world.

Again in Book II, chapter 3, he writes:

He [the monk] must also be obedient to all, so as to learn that he must, as the Lord says, become again a little child, arrogating nothing to himself on the score of his age and the number of the years which he now counts as lost while they were spent to no purpose in the world; and as he is only a beginner, and because of the novelty of the apprenticeship, which he knows he is serving in Christ's service, he should not hesitate to submit himself even to his juniors.

The *Rule of St. Benedict* is unmistakably specific in this matter of age:

The brethren shall take their places according to the date of their conversion, the merit of their lives, or the appointment of their abbot . . . With the exception therefore of those who for some weighty reason, the abbot shall advance or put in a lower place, let all the rest remain in the order of their conversion. For example, one who shall come to the monastery at the second hour of the day shall know that he is junior to him who has come at the first hour, no matter what his age or dignity may be.[82]

---

[82] The *Rule of St. Benedict*, translated with an introduction by Abbot Gasquet, London; 1909, Chap. lxiii, pp. 109, 110.

This custom obtains in religious communities to-day; one's eligibility to office, one's authority and privileges, even one's place at table is determined by one's age in community. Recently I received a letter from a young lady who had been admitted to the novitiate of the Sisters of the Holy Cross, Notre Dame, Indiana. She wrote me after her reception, the day on which she was clothed in the holy habit, "The great day has come and gone and to-day finds me a week and some days old."

If the poet is a young religious, as I have already suggested, and is speaking of heavenly happiness as it is possible to him at this time, he would be thinking of his happiness as a religious. And that state would have only a short period, two years, as he says, on which to reckon a reward.

Again, a novice in a community is considered a child in the religious life and has to learn everything pertaining to his vocation from the beginning. After two years he knows the fundamentals but no more, what one might call the A B C of the spiritual life. Indeed, Cassian uses this expression. He says of the training of the young members by the old: "By these practices, then, they hasten to impress and instruct those whom they are training with the alphabet, as it were, and first syllables in the direction of perfection." (*Institutes,* Book IV, chapter 9.) And when one has quoted Cassian, one has cited the authority *par excellence* on monastic practice; on his *Institutes* St. Benedict based his Rule, which by the end of the eighth century had superseded all others and was "commonly recognized as the code for all monks throughout the West." [83] So when the poet says to the Pearl that she hardly knew a Pater or a Creed he is simply indicating by a familiar figure her extreme youth. Juliana of Norwich constantly speaks of the A B C of spirituality; the reward of youthful service is beautifully referred to in her sixth Revelation:

And I saw that homely and sweetly was this shewed, and that the age of every man shall be [made] known in Heaven, and [he] shall be rewarded for his willing service and for his time. And specially the age of them that willingly and freely offer their youth unto God, passingly is rewarded and wonderfully is thanked.

For I saw that whene'er what time a man or woman is truly turned to God—for one day's service and for his endless will he shall have all these three degrees of bliss. And the more the loving soul seeth the courtesy of God, the liefer he is to serve him all the days of his life (p. 34).

The passage also illuminates the poet's difficulty in reconciling the Maiden's reward with the

---

[83] Cardinal Gasquet, *Monastic Life in the Middle Ages,* p. 205.

shortness of her time in God's service, to which
we shall come presently.   The point, I think, is
not far-fetched, but rather quite obvious to any
one acquainted with the formation or training of
subjects to the monastic life.   The novitiate is
familiarly known as the cradle of the community
and has always been regarded as the nursery of the
religious life.   The Pater Noster and the Creed
are the first prayers learned; they are the fundamental vocal prayers and form an introduction
to most other devotional exercises.   The young
religious commonly begins to learn to meditate,
the fundamental activity of his interior life, by
considering the seven petitions of the Pater Noster
or the twelve articles of the Creed.   Cassian says,
in his first conference, chapters 18-23, entitled
"Of the Lord's Prayer," "And so there follows
. . . a still more sublime condition. . . . And that
we ought . . . to seek after this condition the
formula of the Lord's prayer teaches us," etc.,
after which follows a series of meditations on the
seven petitions.

The practice comes down to our own day; the
Directory of the Sisters of the Holy Cross, a modern community founded in Le Mans, France, in
1836, contains this instruction on the third and
simplest form of mental prayer (meditation):
"It consists in reciting a prayer very slowly; for

instance 'Our Father—who art in heaven—
hallowed be Thy name' and during this breathing
time, to think on the meaning of the words, or the
dignity of the one to whom we pray, or on our
own lowliness" (p. 38). The dashes indicate
pauses of perhaps five minutes or more, during
which the person thinks upon the words just repeated, and their particular application to himself.
"Our Father," for instance, suggests the simplest,
most human, and most tender relation between
God and one's soul. This realization quite naturally stimulates feelings of personal love and
devotion for Him Who is one's Father in an infinite, a divine way. This is, as has been said, the
easiest form of meditation, and is offered to those
who, because of their youth or inexperience or in-
ability, are unable to attempt the more advanced
and difficult methods. When, therefore, the poet
says: "thou . . . never knewest Pater nor Creed,"
he is describing accurately and, one may say,
in the vernacular of religion, a state of spiritual
infancy quite familiar to religious. In the same
breath he is trying to reconcile that state with
the revelation of the reward attached conditionally
to it. He sees his own possible heaven, the
heaven of a youthful virgin soul, and he can
hardly believe the loveliness of it, much less ad-
just his small desert to its munificence. Here is

the crux. The poet speaks almost querulously, deprecatingly as of an injustice; he all but calls the Maiden an impostor. Such an attitude and such speech are quite unthinkable in a father to his dead child and are in no way characteristic of elegiac poetry. On the other hand, they are perfectly congruous with the spiritual hypothesis. They are the scriptural "Lord, I am not worthy" attitude of newly acquired and growing humility. Angela of Foligno says of the beginning of her conversion:

In the fourth place, I began to contemplate and learn the mercy of God, which had extended to me the aforesaid grace. . . . Being thus illuminated, and seeing nothing in myself but defects, I condemned myself, knowing and perceiving most certainly that I was worthy of hell.[84]

And, says Ruysbroeck:

The fourth degree of the Celestial Ladder is true Humility, that is to say, an intimate consciousness of our own baseness! (p. 63).

To establish absolutely the boundlessness of God's reward, out of all proportion to service rendered, the Maiden cites the parable of the Master and the Vineyard, which, she says, "Matthew telleth in your Mass"—the Mass for Septu-

---

[84] Algar Thorold, *Catholic Mysticism*, p. 92.

agesima Sunday. She shows the poet that the Lord has the right, which He exercises despite the murmurs of men, of rewarding with the penny of heavenly beatitude those who have labored but one hour, quite as He does those who have labored the whole day. This, again, would have no application to a child, whose happiness in heaven is a consequence of baptismal innocence and not the reward of a single hour's labor in God's vineyard. But it has an application to the religious in a state of desolation, who "rough, impatient . . . full of . . . useless grief and penal despair," as Cassian says (p. 266), petulantly questions the reasonableness of things generally. Also, it is absolutely consistent with the training and instruction of young religious. It may be remembered that the *Rule of St. Benedict* already quoted uses the figures of the first and second hours of the day, drawn from this parable. Thomas à Kempis advises his novices in his *Sermons* (p. 21) : "Therefore I beseech you, younger ones, listen humbly to the seniors, who have long experience in many things; who have borne in the Order the burden of the day and the heats."

As a matter of fact, the explanation of this parable is one of the first means used in novitiates to make novices understand the discrepancies of age and ability among them. Very early in my

own novitiate, two Sisters died; one, a young
and promising teacher; the other a very old Sister
who had been a cook for many years. Our mistress
of novices used the parable of the vineyard in
speaking of these deaths to us, to impress upon
us that both Sisters had earned, in God's reckon-
ing, their reward, though their time and manner
of working for it had been quite unlike. I cannot overemphasize the frequency with which this
parable enters into religious parlance and daily
conversation. "The eleventh hour" is a collo-
quialism. It sometimes happens that a person enters community rather late in life, at twenty-eight
or thirty years of age, perhaps. His companions
recognize him as a ninth- or eleventh-hour laborer
and have much innocent fun in their merry protests at the prospect of his receiving the same
eternal penny as they who have entered the vineyard at the first hour, the early morning, their
eighteenth or twentieth year. This statement
can be substantiated by no quotation from venerable authorities; it belongs to that part of religious life which does not find its way into print
but which belongs, none the less, to the essence
of community tradition and practice. And the
perfect continuity of practice and spirit that can
be traced in recorded facts ought to support those
that are preserved only in oral tradition. From

this it is evident that *lateness* may refer either to the advanced age of a person entering religious life or the shortness of his time of service, but not to his youth. Hence, when the Vision says:

> Though well-nigh now, I late began,
> at even to the vineyard came. (ll. 581, 582)

she would be understood in religious parlance to imply that she was old when she entered God's vineyard, or had labored only a little while in it. "Euentyde" has the secular connotation of old age—and if applied to a *daughter*, Pearl, would mean that she had died an old woman, a completely untenable reading of the line.[85]

This *Pearl* poet is an extremely hard-headed man; he tells the Maiden that her tale seems "reasonless"; if one laborer worked all the day and she, but lately arrived, has come to payment

---

[85] The interpretations of the Parable of the Laborers in the Vineyard with which the *Pearl* poet could have been familiar are those of St. John Chrysostom, in *Homilies*, pp. 64 and 64, also *Post Nicene Fathers*, Vol. X, p. 393.

St. Cyrillus of Alexandria, in Homilies, p. 77.

St. Augustine, Sermon 37 in *Post Nicene Fathers*, Vol. VI, p. 373.

The fundamental idea of the parable as understood by St. Jerome, Albertus Magnus, Thomas Aquinas is that God apportions reward according to the merits of faith, which depends on grace. Such an interpretation could have no application to the Vision if she were a child two years old, for at that age she would not have the use of reason with which to correspond with grace or to practice faith.

before him, then "the less the work, the more the pay." Now, is it for a moment conceivable that a heart-sick father would stand and quibble and split hairs in this fashion, begrudging the child for whom he is mourning the degree of happiness that has been granted her? But an over-wrought, disconsolate religious would be quite capable of this. It is to such a one that Thomas à Kempis says: "Fear the judgments of God; dread the anger of the Almighty; but presume not to examine the works of the Most High" (*Imitation,* III. 4).

The Vision insists that there is no debate with Christ between more and less; He pours His gifts on all. She concludes:

> Large is His freedom who hath fear'd
> 'fore Him that rescueth in sin;
> no bliss shall be withheld from such. (ll. 609-611)

Clearly, this is the freedom implied in St. Augustine's "Love God and do what you please"; it is the liberty of the converted and repentant man. A child of two can hardly know, much less fear God to any salutary end, or exercise the liberty arising from such fear. The Maiden realizes that she is engaged in religious controversy, and anticipates the poet's further objection to her reward by asking:

Where knewest thou any man abide,
ever so holy in his prayer,
who ne'er, in some way, forfeited
the meed, sometime, of heaven bright? (ll. 617-620)

The poet must be judging here by the standards of restored, rather than baptismal innocence, else she would not seek her justification from examples of older persons who, however holy, have suffered some diminution of virtue and hence of reward. She never identifies her condition with that proper to a child.

In fact, she continues to explain that through the water of baptism children are saved, refers to them in the third person, *they,* and speaks of "Death's might" to which *they* bow as something entirely remote from her. And in the stanza immediately preceding she has been talking of "my penny," and "I . . . am not worth so great a wage" in comparison with the active members in God's vineyard. She lays no emphasis on the reward of infants without any merit of their own, but merely states that the grace of God is sufficient to justify it—she who has been at such pains to explain her own reward as in some manner connected with activity in the service of God. Here, among baptized children the poet should find his daughter or at least some reference to her,

but there is absolutely none.   The Vision puts
herself in another group of souls altogether.
    She says further:

> two kinds to save is good and just—
> the righteous man . . .
> the harmless one. (ll. 673-675)

and adds significantly:

> So when thou comest to the Court,
> where all our causes shall be cried,
>
> .   .   .   .   .   .
>
> He that bloodily died on rood,
>
> .   .   .   .   .   .
>
> grant thee to pass, when tried thou art
> by innocence and not by right. (ll. 701-708)

From which it is evident that the poet is to be
saved by the grace of redemption and not by the
right of baptism, and that it is his state of soul
in which both the Maiden and himself are concerned.   This is not an elegiac attitude.   It is the
constantly recurring theme of spiritual autobiography.
    She continues on the subject of childhood, re-
ferring to our Lord's glorification of it in bid-
ding little children to come to Him, but still without including herself among them.   She explains
that

> no man might win His realm
> save he come thither as a child. (ll. 722-723)

Now, if the poet is seeking his dead daughter, this is rather indirect advice for him, and no consolation whatever. But if he is lamenting a lost state of spiritual joy, the counsel to become as a little child is ideal and perfect. Spiritual childhood is the goal toward which all religious training tends; it is the one trustful, confiding attitude in which the soul rests entirely in God and finds complete consolation in Him. Juliana says in her *Revelations:*

He (Christ) willeth then that we use the condition of a child. . . . And if He sees that it be more profit to us to mourn and to weep, He suffereth it, with ruth and pity, unto the best time, for love. (p. 154)

There, the Maiden continues,

is the bliss that cannot fade,
the jeweller sought 'mong precious gems,
and sold his all . . .
to purchase him a spotless pearl.

This spotless pearl, so dearly bought,

is like the realm of heaven's sphere;

for it is flawless, bright, and pure,
endless round, of lustre blithe,
and common to all that righteous were. (ll. 729-744)

Here, from one who has authority to speak, is a definition of a pearl which can be applied only to a state of spiritual happiness, and not to a child. Here is a justification of the description of the poet's pearl in the first stanza, "so round . . . so smooth," but not an identification of it with a child. The realm of heaven is a sphere as is the pearl; it is flawless, bright, pure, lustrous, as is a pearl. Obviously a child is neither flawless, lustrous, nor spherical.

Then, pointing to herself, she says: "Lo, its setting amid my breast" (l. 740). It is the great dramatic gesture, the climactic moment of the entire poem. It is the key to the interpretation. The pearl, corresponding in every detail to that lost by the poet, is found; it is set in the breast of this heavenly Maiden. Therefore, the Maiden is not his pearl, and the pearl is not a child. It is "like the realm of Heaven's sphere," she says, and then continues:

> My Lord the Lamb——
> He set it there in token of peace.
> I rede thee forsake the world wild,
> and get for thee thy spotless pearl. (ll. 741-744)

This is not the language of elegy or lament. But it is precisely the language of spiritual formation. Even after a person has entered a community, he retains by habit if not by desire, much of the world that he has left. This he is constantly enjoined to relinquish, to be rid of wholly. Cassian gives this warning: "Beware therefore lest at any time you take again any of those things which you renounced and forsook . . . neither sink back to desires of this world" (*Institutes,* p. 231), and Thomas à Kempis almost paraphrases the Pearl's advice: "Convert thyself with thy whole heart to the Lord, and quit this miserable world, and thy soul shall find rest" (*Imitation,* II. 1). The world cannot possibly present the dangers to a secular person that it does to a religious; pleasures legitimate to the former are perilous, if not sinful to the latter. The injunction to become as little children was addressed to all men, but only those who wished to follow Christ along the evangelical paths of perfection, under vows of poverty, chastity, and obedience are counseled to forsake the world. This admonition, if given by a daughter to her father, seems to fail in its application. On the other hand it dovetails perfectly into the following stanzas on the religious vocation. One ought to remark here that the Maiden bids the poet "get for thee *thy* spotless pearl." This, again, establishes her identity as distinct from the pearl he is seeking.

The poet recognizes this and asks:

O spotless Pearl——

.   .   .   .   .   .

who form'd for thee thy figure fair?

.   .   .   .   .   .

thy beauty never from Nature came;
Pygmalion painted ne'er thy face;
nor Aristotle, with all his lore,
told of the qualities of these gifts. (ll. 745-751)

This is a declaration of the supernatural character of the Vision; nature, ancient art, or philosophy could not account for such beauty, such
gifts. They must be entirely spiritual, altogether
heavenly. The very robe in which the spotless
Pearl was clad was the work of one "full wise";
her very bearing had the mark of divinity upon
it. This Maiden is the fruit of grace; no human
power, no natural force could have produced her.
An infant is the result of these; human beauty
owed its debt to Pygmalion, and human wisdom
acknowledges its obligation to Aristotle. But a
soul in the state of sanctifying grace, that is, as
it will be in heaven, is radiant beyond these, not
merely in degree, but in kind. No artifice of
human device can produce this *kind* of beauty.
The poet simply is not dealing with natural causes
or natural results; he is speaking of a supernatural state as he sees it realized in his vision, and
he says so. And then comes the poet's tremendous
question:

Tell me, Brightest, what is the peace
that beareth as token this spotless pearl? (ll. 755, 756)

The pearl is a token, a symbol of peace; the poet
is not seeking a child but a state, a condition of
peace, symbolized by a pearl. In answer to this
direct question, the Maiden answers:

My spotless Lamb

. . . . . .

chose me His bride, though all unfit
the Spousal might a while well seem. (ll. 757-760)

which is the simplest and commonest expression
of one's election to the religious life. The pearl
for which the poet is seeking is, as I have said,
found in the religious life, upon the word of the
poet's own Vision.

The line "when I went forth from your wet
world" (761) may seem to imply death but it is
an expression regularly used to indicate entrance
into the religious life. The *Imitation* says:

Be vigilant . . . and often think . . . to what end
thou camest hither and why thou didst leave the world.
(I. 25)

Her attributes, the Maiden says, are from her
Spouse:

He gave me strength and beauty too;
and crown'd clean in maidenhood,
in His blood on the Throne He wash'd my weeds;
with spotless pearls He me beset. (ll. 765-768)

The parallel of this passage with *Juliana* is very close:

He is our clothing, that for love wrappeth us and windeth us, halseth us, and all becloseth us, hangeth about us for tender love, that He may never leave us (*op. cit.,* p. 38).

And with this our good Lord said well blessed fully: "Lo, how I love thee," as if He has said: "My darling, behold and see the Lord thy God is thy Maker and thy endless joy. See thine own Brother, thy Saviour. My child, behold and see what liking and bliss I have in thy salvation; and for my love enjoy with Me" (p. 32).

Thomas à Kempis says to his novices, in his *Sermons* (p. 83):

And if you cannot yet understand or grasp the joys to come prepared in the heavenly nuptials, nevertheless believe that God is faithful to give what He has promised to them that love Him.

Cassian knits up the two ideas implied in the Pearl situation, that of recovered childhood in the religious and of vocation, thus, in speaking of the religious habit:

For they . . . use very small hoods . . . in order that they may constantly be moved to preserve the simplicity and innocence of little children. . . . And these men have returned to childhood in Christ.

However, this nuptial relation of the virgin soul to Christ is too fundamental a part of the religious and social organization of the Christian world to need the support of such abundant quotation as one might easily offer.

Critics may have a difficulty out of

Come hither to Me, My truelove sweet,
For stain or spot is none in thee. (ll. 763, 764)

as representing an immaculateness that even the grace of God in repentance could not restore to the soul. It stands in the text apparently as a loose quotation from the Canticle of Canticles, IV, 7: "Thou art all fair, O my love, and there is not a spot in thee"; which text, by the way, does not imply the innocence of infancy. One finds the expression in "Of Clean Maidenhood," to mention only one of numerous mediæval lyrics in which it occurs.

The unworthiness of the Bride for her high vocation implied in stanza lxv is an experience that every religious has undergone; God's love of predilection which has selected and chosen him from among so many is an enveloping wonder to him, a source of endless gratitude and humility.

And it has not the remotest connection with the spirit or tradition of elegiac poetry.

There remains the transcendant climax of the poet's dream. It is the Maiden's exposition of heaven, a paraphrase of the Apocalypse. There is no need to review the details of it. But this is significant; the Vision describes the heaven of virgins. As has already been said, Professor Schofield's comment on this is surprisingly myopic; he does not draw the obvious conclusion that the writer must have been a person who had taken the vow of chastity. One would scarcely employ the precious moments of vision in describing to the favored ecstatic a condition from which he, by his very relation to the heavenly visitant, was excluded. The most conveniently adjustable interpretation will not claim for a two-year-old child, no matter in what maturity of glorified beatitude, a state of happiness dependent on deliberate choice, postulating deliberate renunciation. No heaven, even of research, could be more ironical. Or, supposing the poet to be the father of the girl of his vision, legitimate or illegitimate, the revelation could have been at best an impossibility, and at worst a burning reproach. Plainly it was neither; it melted him to madness, drove him into an ecstasy of delight—his own word for it. Another difficulty here: had the Pearl been an illegitimate child, as Professor Schofield suggests,[86] she would have been debarred from entering a religious community (illegitimacy constituting an impediment) and an exposition on the heaven of virgins from her mouth would have been the cheapest of travesties.

Olympia, the dead daughter of Silvius in Boccaccio's *Olympia,* returns to her father in a dream and describes to him a heaven almost identical in detail with that which the *Pearl* poet enjoys. She enumerates the different Orders or Companies of the blessed; she names and describes the band of virgin souls and after them the host of children among whom she dwells. She says:

> Agmon adest niveum post hos, cui lilia frontes
> Circumdant, huic juncta cohors tua pulchra manemus
> Natorum.

> Then come the Snow-white Host; lilies their brows
> enwreathe. To these is joined our little band,
> thy children fair.
> > Edited with *Pearl,* by I. Gollancz, 280.

She recognizes and mentions the distinction between the virgin souls and those of children in heaven. The Maiden does not mention children in her heaven at all, but devotes all her details of description to the company of virgins. If she

---

[86] "Nature and Fabric of the Pearl," *Publications of the Modern Language Association,* Vol. XIX, pp. 154-215.

had been a child she could not have done this
consistently.

Her speech now is all of the New Jerusalem,
her description of her Jewel, her Lamb, is that
of

> the Glorious Guiltless whom they killed,
>
> .   .   .   .   .   .
> As a sheep to the slaughter was He led. (ll. 800-802)

the Isaian vision of the Crucified. This follows
precisely the lines of spiritual autobiography;
especially is it the consolation of a desolate soul.
One finds in the ninth Revelation of Juliana
(p. 47):

> In this feeling my understanding was lifted up into
> Heaven, and there I saw three heavens. . . .
> For the First Heaven, Christ shewed me His Father;
> in no bodily likeness, but in His property and in His
> working. The first heaven shewed to me as one heaven;
> and it was full blissful; for He is full pleased with all
> the deeds that Jesus hath done about our salvation. This
> that I say is so great bliss to Jesus that He setteth at
> naught all His travail, and His hard Passion, and His
> cruel death.

This very mystic glorification of the Passion
the Maiden also explains:

> But none would doubt the Lamb's delight;
> though He were hurt and wounded sore,
> none could it in His semblance see,
> His glance so glorious was and glad. (ll. 1140-1144)

The eulogy on the passion was a favorite theme of mediæval poetry as it was of spiritual autobiography. It constitutes the eight, ninth, and tenth of Juliana's *Revelations;* it constitutes the fourteenth and fifteenth chapters of the *Book of Eternal Wisdom;* it comprises the seventh, eighth, ninth, and tenth steps in the Conversion of Angela of Foligno; one finds it the subject of the eleventh and twelfth chapters of the second book of the *Imitation of Christ.*

The Vision goes further to say that each pure soul is a wife to the Lamb; a view expressed also by Suso, "My dwelling is in the pure soul as in a paradise of delights." Eternal Wisdom also answers his question, so like the poet's own:

My Lord, what manner of place is my fatherland? Or what do people there? Or are there very many people there? Or do they really know so well what takes place with us on earth as Thy words declare? [87]

To this last she says:

And though our corses cling in clay,
and ye for ruth cry ceaselessly,
we knowledge have full well of this—
from one death cometh all our hope,
Us gladdeneth the Lamb. (ll. 857-862)

The elegiac interpretation of the poem may very well claim justification in the first two of

---

[87] *Little Book of Eternal Wisdom,* p. 77.

the lines just quoted. They seem to indicate clearly that the Maiden speaking has been buried, has been mourned for to excess. But one must remember that here she is speaking of the happiness of all the saved, the bliss of all in heaven. Lament over the dead is general, as she observes; but likewise all hope in heaven comes from one death, that of the Lamb. This is a general truth and not an elaboration upon the death of any particular person. The use of the plurals, "our," "we," "us," emphasizes this. Also, the Maiden says, "ye cry ruthlessly," addressing people generally, whose attitude toward death she is describing. She is not speaking to the poet particularly, for in addressing him, she always says "thou." She does so in the first line of the next stanza, making the change from the general audience to the particular person unquestionable:

But lest thou deem my tale less true. (l. 865)

And in speaking to the poet she falls back directly to St. John's apocalyptic vision of the hundred and forty-four thousand virgins with the name of the Lamb "on all their foreheads writ." This is the proof of veracity that she offers him; this is his particular hope and consolation. For "ye" that mourn over death there is the hope of redemption through the death of the Lamb; but for "thou," the poet, there is the vision of the heaven of virgins. It is almost impossible to regard the poet as anything but a religious under all of these circumstances.

And such a very human religious, too. He is still worried about sensible joys, despite the obloquy heaped upon the senses by his Vision. He confesses that he is "but earth and dust awhile" (l. 905) and so wants to see the houses and walls within which this Maiden dwells. He is going to take no chances on Paradisal changes in the weather; " 'twere perilous to lodge without" (l. 930); then, too, so great a host of souls must occupy "a city vast" (l. 928). One might poke fun at his very unmystical attitude.

> Where I tarry by these banks,
> I see no dwelling anywhere. (ll. 931, 932)

He is still concerned with tangible comfort, sensible security of happiness. He is the very pattern of a religious who places his joy in natural spiritual sweetness; he cannot yet contemplate a supreme happiness which is a state rather than a place, which is free from material elements and yet infinitely perfect without them. He still hankers for the sensible and the accidental, as he did in the beginning of his dream. From the vision of this utterly spiritual heaven he is de-

barred, "God this forbiddeth," the Maiden tells
him:

> but from the Lamb I welcome thee
> to a sight thereof, by His great grace. (ll. 967, 968)

and now his foolishness and slowness of heart are
illumined, his spiritual eyes are opened to behold
from afar the uttermost beauties of the New
Jerusalem, as described in the Apocalypse. It is
a moment of utter ecstasy. He is mad, shaken
with delight, wrapt completely out of himself.
He has experienced in dream the ineffabilities of
true interior joy; he has seen, in all the transcen-
dencies of its sheer spirituality, his pearl with
the eyes of his soul. He is no longer a man to
be wedded to sensible consolations or to wax disconsolate over their loss. He has not only com-
prehended but has learned the lesson of the *Pearl*.
And so he wakes.

We said earlier in this study, and justified the
statement by abundant and consistent citations,
that the *Pearl* poet was a man evidently suffering from spiritual depression, or at least recording such an experience, and that persons actually in that state are ordinarily directed to rely
on the grace of God, the merits of Christ, and
after that are invariably recommended to con-

sider the happiness of heaven as an ultimate and sufficient reward. So true is this that a common expression among religious is, "Heaven is worth it all." "What is this compared to eternity," was the favorite aspiration of St. Aloysius. Meditation on heaven is an ordinary means that religious have practiced, from the beginning of monasticism, to help them bear patiently the crosses of this life. Thomas à Kempis has chapters on the consideration of heaven. These quotations from chapters 47, 48, and 49 of the third book will suffice.

Son, be not dismayed with the labors which thou hast undertaken for Me; neither let the tribulations which befall thee quite cast thee down; but let My promise strengthen thee, and comfort thee in all events. . . .

Mind what thou art about; labor faithfully in My vineyard; I will be thy reward.

Write, read, sing, sigh, keep silence, pray, bear thy crosses manfully: eternal life is worthy of all these, and greater combats.

Are not all painful labors to be endured for everlasting life?

O most happy mansion of the city above! O most bright day of eternity . . . a day always joyful, always secure, and never changing its state for the contrary.

When shall I enjoy a solid peace never to be disturbed, and always secure, a peace both within and without, and a peace every way firm?

O good Jesus, when shall I stand to behold Thee?

When shall I contemplate the glory of Thy kingdom? O when shall I be with Thee in Thy kingdom?

Comfort me in my banishment, assuage my sorrow; for all my desire is after Thee.

But consider, son, the fruit of these labors, how quickly they will end, and their exceeding great reward, and thou wilt not be troubled at them, but strongly comforted in thy suffering.

For in regard to that little of thy will which thou now forsakest thou shalt forever have thy will in heaven.

This preoccupation with heaven is not the habit of laymen and has not been conspicuously so at any time. Even poets have not glorified elegiac poetry with the splendor of such a hope. Secular writers of the fourteenth century were imitating the *Romaunt of the Rose* much more assiduously than they were paraphrasing the book of *Revelations*. Wherefore again, I conclude that the *Pearl* is a bit of spiritual autobiography from the pen of a religious.

3. THE "PEARL" INTERPRETED BY THE TEXT ITSELF

This tedious stanza by stanza discussion of the text has ruined perspective on the poem and has partially obscured the theme. But having in this dull fashion established an alibi in spiritual autobiography, in the literature of interior desolation, for every declared doctrine and every state of soul therein described, I can now lift the *Pearl*-poet story out its beautiful and consistent elaboration and let it explain itself. It runs thus:

Poet: I placed my Pearl apart, supreme.
      I lost it . . . in a garden . . . alas!

      .   .   .   .   .   .

      I pine . . . despoiled
      of Pearl mine own. (ll. 7-12)

(He sleeps and in a dream sees a spotless child bedight with pearls standing on the bank of a stream opposite him. He speaks.)

Poet: Art thou my Pearl, that I have plained? (l. 242)

Pearl: What thou didst lose was but a rose,
      that flower'd and fail'd, as Nature bade;
      through the casket's grace, enclosing it,
      it now is proved a pearl of price. (ll. 269-272)

(She then explains the consistency of heavenly rewards, using the parable of the vineyard as illustration, with emphasis on the point that sometimes short service is recompensed more quickly and abundantly than long years of labor. She discriminates between the reward of this short labor and that of baptised infants. She extols the innocence of childhood, and says:)

Pearl: Jesus . . . said, no man might win His realm
      save he came thither as a child;

      .   .   .   .   .   .

      There is the bliss that cannot fade,
      the jeweller sought 'mong precious gems,
      and sold his all . . .
      to purchase him a spotless pearl.

"This spotless pearl . . .
is like the realm of Heaven's sphere";
so saith the Father. . . .
Lo, its setting amid my breast!
My Lord the Lamb, who shed His blood,
He set it there in token of peace.
I rede thee forsake the world so wild,
and get for thee thy spotless pearl. (ll. 721-744)

Poet: Tell me, Brightest, what is the peace
that bearest as token this spotless pearl?
(ll. 755, 756)

Pearl: My spotless Lamb . . .
chose me His bride, though all unfit
the Spousal might a while well seem.

.   .   .   .   .   .

He gave me strength and beauty too;
.   .   .   .   .   .

and, crowned clean with maidenhood,
with spotless pearls He me beset.

.   .   .   .   .   .

We all in bliss are Brides of the Lamb,
a hundred and forty-four thousand in all,
as in the Apocalypse it is clear. (ll. 757-787)

(A description of the heavenly Jerusalem follows, in
which the poet shares St. John's vision, and sees the
Maiden a crowned queen among virgins. He wakes and
says:)

Poet: Over yon mound I had this hap,
prone there for pity of my Pearl,
to God I then committed it,
in Christ's dear blessing and mine own—
Christ that in form of bread and wine
the priest each day to us doth shew;

He grant we be His servants leal—
yea, precious Pearls to please Him aye!
            Amen. Amen.

Here is the key to the poem, the interpretation of the allegory. The pearl is, according to the Maiden's word, like heaven, and can be gained only by those who have become, through grace, like little children spiritually. It is a token of peace; this peace she enjoys as a Bride of the Lamb who has espoused her. This explanation, contained in the text itself, cannot possibly have reference to a dead baby. It is of the very essence of the religious life. The ultimate motive for which every sincere religious leaves his secular state is the more secure hope of heaven. He is reborn, as it were, in his community; he enters into a state of spiritual infancy which it is his ambition to retain to the end of his life. He enjoys therein peace which, with his spiritual growth and development, becomes increasingly profound and interior. It rests on his complete union with God, his unquestioning trust in Him, his uncomplaining resignation to whatever befalls him, accidentally, provided only the purity of his soul be not compromised. He looks forward to a state of immortality in which he will be espoused to Christ, not in the general sense in which every pure soul is His beloved, but in that more intimate union indicated by St. John as proper to the hundred and forty-four thousand who were virgins and who follow the Lamb whithersoever He goeth.

The Maiden has chosen in her exposition, not a single detail that is peculiar and exclusively proper to the secular state, or to infancy; she has enumerated those identical with religious life and applicable only to it. It seems abundantly clear that she is talking of a state of soul of a religious; that she herself represents a religious state; that she is talking to a religious person. Moreover, the poet is completely satisfied with her revelations. He has been bewailing his pearl, his hope of heaven; but he will do so no more. Rather he will trust his future to Christ, Christ in the Blessed Sacrament, praying that we all may be precious pearls to Him—as Juliana says, "We be His crown."

His state of spiritual desolation and interior dryness has passed; his rough impatience, his over-confidence in sensible comfort, in proofs from reason, his incipient despair have all been sweetly replaced by a most gentle patience, a profound humility, and a childlike docility to his Prince. It is a "consummation devoutly to be wished," a perfect conclusion to this little drama of a soul's nostalgia.

The allegory of the *Pearl* has yet to be simplified. Because of what one might call "the pearl note" running through the poem, the reader encounters some difficulty in keeping distinct the Pearl child, the poet's pearl, token of heaven, and pearls used in costume and atmosphere. The pearl, token of heaven, is a figure used by the Maiden to symbolize her state of purity and bliss. It is practically identical with that state. The pearls used in the general setting of the poem are the jewels that adorn the Maiden's robe, those that bestrew the river shore, and others that the poet uses in crowns and raiment to repeat, in every manner of adaptation, the idea, pearl. The Pearl child, I hold, represents the poet's own soul, as it might be in a state of perfection at this particular time of his life. I think this because her condition is so well documented, so to say; she is nearer to him than aunt or niece, her years in God's service he has counted accurately, her proficiency in matters of prayer he knows in intimate detail. Her state is that of spiritual childhood, of absolute and confirmed happiness, in the heaven of virgins. Internal evidence indicates that the author of *Pearl* was a religious; all of these details can be applied to no one so properly as to him. The matters of age can, indeed, be referred to a child, but the heaven of a child is not the heaven of this Pearl, whereas the state of infancy here indicated can be and always has been predicted of young religious. The very constant and personal concern of this Pearl for the poet's actual spiritual state confirms me in regarding her as the visualization of his soul's desired perfection. She actually scolds him into a more confiding faith, more complete humility, and resignation in her three reprimands; she counsels him to become as a little child; she advises him to "leave the world," an idiom in religious life for the complete relinquishing of all things apart from God. Who, more than one's own potentially perfect soul, would be apt to propose such a course of conduct? Surely not an infant daughter.

The poet's pearl is his hope of heaven, of the Beatific Vision, the greatest spiritual consolation that a person can have. He has evidently felt a sensible exuberance in his anticipation of immortality, as is most common among young religious. He has felt it as an actual possession and has taken what he considered a holy joy in it. The consolations of God rather than the God of consolations have beguiled him. Then disaster befalls him. He looses the sensible sweetness of this hope. He does not know where it has gone. It has slipped from him, this jewel, and disappeared. He is at a loss to know what to do without it, yet no amount of railing against Providence will restore it. He, indeed, has not lost faith in God, the supreme Heaven of his desires, but he no longer feels any relish in serving Him. He has lost that sweetness, that delight. He is dry, utterly desolate. He continues in that condition until the real state of his soul, as made possible through grace, is revealed to him. Then his pearl, his hope of heaven, is restored to him; not now, indeed, subject to the childishness of sensible devotion, but entrusted unconditionally to the loving Providence of God. This is not a distortion of the allegory but a very consistent reading of it; it is entirely in accord with the Catholic spirit of the poem and the religious life which it obviously pictures.

4. LITERARY PARALLELS TO "PEARL"

Fully as important as the fact that *Pearl* yields itself in every particular to an interpretation of spiritual desolation is this other fact that it is one of a group of such autobiographies with which it can be closely paralleled. It is no part of my task to trace the history of spiritual confessions; I shall indicate such outstanding examples as during the thirteenth and fourteenth centuries kept

company with *Pearl*. There is the beautiful
Soliloquium attributed to St. Bonaventure, a conversation between Anima and Homo, which begins with the proposition: [88]

"Quomodo anima per mentale exercitium debit
radium, contemplationis reflectere ad interiora
sua, ut videat qualiter est formata per naturam,
deformata per culpam, et reformata per gra-
tiam"; the long, long lesson in *Pearl,* and concludes in precisely the dispositions of the poet
at the end of his contemplation: "Oro, Deus
meus, cognoscam te, amen te, ut aeternaliter
gaudeam de te. Et si non possum ad plenum in
hac vita, crescat saltem hic notitia et amor, ut
ibi sit plenum gaudium; hic sit in spe, et ibi sit
in re." The intervening dialogue has been devoted to a consideration of sin, of the grace of
God, of the passion of Christ, of the miseries of
life, of the greatness of heaven, and of the pre-
eminence of the Blessed Virgin among the blessed:
practically the same subjects discussed in *Pearl*
and in almost the same sequence. If one were
embarrassed by a paucity of material, one might
make much of these resemblances. There are,
however, at least three other studies of the in-

---

[88] Giovanni de Fidanza Bonaventure, *Opera Omnia,* Paris,
1864, Vol. XII, p. 87.

terior life in which the parallelism with *Pearl* is so striking as to amount almost to conclusive evidence for the spiritual interpretation of the poem.

The first is *The Book of the Lover and the Beloved* by Ramon Lull and is dated approximately 1260. It may easily have been known in England in the middle of the fourteenth century, as Lull was living in Paris in 1303, and according to one story, "is said to have been enticed to England in the summer of 1305 by King Edward I." [89] It is a superlatively mystical prose poem, in which all of the experience of the English poet and more pours itself out in ardent beauty from the burning heart of this blessed and romantic "fool of God." This is the story of his soul as he himself tells it.

By verdant paths, with feeling, imagination, understanding, and will the Lover went in search of his Beloved. And in those paths the Lover endured griefs and perils for his Beloved's sake, that he might lift up his will and understanding to his Beloved, who wills that His lovers may comprehend and love Him exceedingly. (p. 97)

The Lover lost a jewel which he greatly prized, and

---

[89] R. Lull, *The Book of the Lover and the Beloved,* translated from the Catalan by E. Allison Peers, New York, 1923. Introduction, Note 1, 7.

was sorely distressed, until his Beloved put to him this question: Which profiteth thee more, the jewel that thou hast lost or thy patience in all the acts of thy Beloved? (p. 105)

The Lover fell asleep while thinking on the trials and the obstacles which he met in serving his Beloved; and he feared lest through those hindrances his works might be lost; but the Beloved sent consciousness to him, and he awakened to the merits and powers of his Beloved. (p. 106)

Full of tears and anguish the Lover went in search of his Beloved, by the path of the senses and also by the intellectual road. Which of those two, think you, did he enter first, as he went after his Beloved? And in which of them did the Beloved reveal Himself to him the more openly? (p. 108)

There is no question at all but that Ramon Lull's book is a spiritual autobiography for he exclaims in the ardor of his confessions:

O Beloved, who in one name, Jesus Christ, art called both God and Man, by that name my will seeks to adore Thee as God and Man. And if Thou, Beloved, hast so greatly honoured Thy Lover, through none of his merits, why honourest Thou not so many ignorant men, who knowingly had been less guilty of dishonouring Thy name, Jesus Christ, than has Thy Lover? (p. 99).

Christ and his soul are the *dramatis personæ* of the action here depicted; the soul seeks this Beloved through sensible avenues and suffers exceedingly in order that he might arrive at a more perfect understanding of the real love of Christ. He loses a precious jewel, and learns through the loss the lesson of patience and complete resignation to God's will. He falls asleep through sheer weariness and trouble of soul over his loss of spiritual sweetness; he fears that he has forfeited his claims to Christ's good pleasure. But with returning consciousness he comes to the truer understanding of the merits and powers of God, which, without such experience, he could not have so well appreciated. He sought both the consolations of God ("by the path of the senses") and the God of consolations ("by the intellectual road"); and the rhetorical question with which the writer concludes this statement leaves the reader to infer that he found Him by the latter.

The parallel with the introduction and conclusion of the *Pearl* is almost perfect. Just a glance at the closeness, the richness, and the significance of the resemblances makes the findings of research on the poet-father and the Pearl-child appear meager, overworked, and far-fetched. One might make a chart of their likenesses, thus:

Book of Lover and Beloved	*Pearl*
Setting: "verdant paths"	Setting: "in on erbere"
Characters: Lover / Beloved	Characters: Poet / Pearl
Action: Loss of jewel / Sore distress	Action: Loss of pearl / Woe and bitter complaints
Sleep / Awakening to a realization of "merits and powers of his Beloved"	Sleep / Awakening to complete resignation. "Now al be to that Prynces paye."

Scenery and Costumes: Consummate and almost identical symbolism and allegory, *e. g.*:

"a delightful meadow—flowers—the casement of love."	"magic of wondrous hills—birds—and plants and spice and fruit."
"vest, and mantle—and helmet of love,"	"Gleaming white was her surcoat fine—nobly edged with pearls."

Out of the north of Wales comes, in the middle of the thirteenth century this other bit of mystic autobiography. It is a page from the diary of another intimate lover of God. The writer is practically unknown except for these fragments. He is identified with a parish priest, Iorwerth Dhu, who went on the third Crusade, and on his return, retired into seclusion and study in his little parish in North Wales. His transcriptions of old manuscripts, some fragments on the Sacraments and the Mass, and this exquisite bit, "The Christian's Way," are all contained in one volume preserved in the National Library at Aberystwyth. His story runs thus:

In a fair castle crowning a lofty mountain dwelt my Love (Christ). Fairer than all other castles in the world was this one, and beautiful the gardens and pleasaunces within its walls.

Weary of war, tired of the din of strife . . . I lay down one day to rest from the heat of the sun, and straightway came to my mind the vision of the castle of my first Love. Many days I journeyed, impatient to draw near the castle. A fellow traveller . . . did say: "When thou drawest nigh unto thy Love, He will turn from thee." . . . At this I became sorrowful, and presently I saw that our path no longer led upwards, nor in the direction of the castle, but down towards a gloomy chasm. Then would my heart freeze, but my soul fiercely cried, "Thy Love is waiting, still waiting." At the same moment . . . I saw a brief glimpse of my Love's banner waving in the bright sunshine beyond the valley. By so much the nearer I drew to the castle, so grew it

fairer to my eyes, and at length I beheld my Love, standing in the gateway, radiant in the sunshine that shone on
His face and glittered on the rubies that adorned Him.
"Help, Lord, or I shall surely perish, for of excess of
love I shall die at beholding Thy face," I cried as I fell
to the ground as one dead. When I returned to myself
I saw my Love still waiting for me, but to my wonder
He pointed out a winding, narrow rugged path which
was soon lost in the woods, instead of the straight and
spacious road leading to the castle. Filled with ardour
I ran forward upon this broad way . . . but suddenly
I saw that the road was washed away to a deep ravine.
After much climbing I found the path which my Love
had pointed to me, which I followed with joy, wherein
also do I now continue by His gracious mercy, until I
shall pass through this darkness to the brightness beyond,
where I shall possess my Love forever.[90]

Here, again, is a similar identity of setting,
characters, and action:

Crusader	*Poet*
"weary of war, tired of strife."	"Care full cold seized on me; a senseless moan dinned in my heart."
"I lay down to rest."	"I fell upon that flowery plot. I slid into a slumber-swoon."

---

[90] Monsignor P. E. Hook, "A Mediæval Welsh Mystic,"
Dublin Review, July 1924, pp. 21-28.

"Straightway came to my mind the vision of the castle of my first Love."

"My soul . . . fared adventuring, where marvels be. Methought that Paradise lay beyond . . . the castle-bounds . . . were marked."

"I journeyed, impatient to draw near the castle."

"There sat a child . . . a maid of grace. Were I with thee . . . I were a joyful jeweller."

Here follows a description of interior desolation comparable to the experience of the poet. Both men have this glimpse of the new Jerusalem.

"I stood—dazed—in wonder of that gladsome sight, —ravished by that radiance. The Lamb their lantern that never fail'd."

"The nearer I drew to the castle, so grew it fairer.—I beheld my Love, radiant in the sunshine—"

Both visions reach the breaking point at the exquisiteness of joy in the ineffable delights of God's love. Both men wake in possession of Christ's abiding friendship, humbly resolved to accept His will, and confidently hopeful of His everlasting possession.

Henry Suso's *Little Book of Eternal Wisdom*

furnishes a third intimate study of the interior life, along lines parallel with *Pearl*. The little volume has already done gallant service in particular stanza comparisons; it presents as convincing a resemblance to the poem when taken *in toto* as in isolated passages. Whereas Lull regarded the condition of spiritual desolation with the emotional vaccilation of an almost combustible lover, and the retired Crusader with the rugged composure of a Welsh fighter, Henry Suso brought to his encounter with interior dryness both the unsophistication of his life and the native mysticism of his temperament. His report of experiences is naturally the most unworldly of the three. It is likewise less worldly, though not more subtle than *Pearl*. It is, briefly, as follows:

A Servant was filled with disgust and dejection of heart on his first setting forth on the uneven ways. Then did the Eternal Wisdom meet him in spiritual and ineffable form, and lead him through bitter and sweet until she brought him to the right path of divine truth (p. 24).

This vision of Eternal Wisdom Suso describes in his *Life* as a surpassingly beautiful girl, "under a lovely guise, as a gracious loving mistress . . . discoursing the while, in female form" (p. 11).

Eternal Wisdom: Now open thy interior eyes and see who I am. It is I, Eternal Wisdom, who, with the embrace of my eternal providence, have chosen thee in eternity for Myself alone.

The Servant: Tender loving Wisdom! And is it Thou I have so long been seeking for? Is it thou my spirit has so constantly struggled for? Alas, my God, why didst Thou not show Thyself to me long ago?

Eternal Wisdom: Had I done so thou wouldst not have known My goodness so sensibly as now thou knowest it. . . . My unfathomable love shows itself in the great bitterness of My passion like the sun in its brightness, like the fair rose in its perfume (pp. 26-28).

There follows a divine exposition of the Passion, the essence of which is:

Eternal Wisdom: No one enjoys Me more in My singular sweetness than he who stands with Me in harshness and bitterness. . . . No one complains so much of the bitterness of the husks as he to whom the interior sweetness of the kernel is unknown (p. 32).

Upon being thus interiorly illuminated the Servant speaks:

The Servant: Lord, Thy countenance is so full of graciousness. Thy mouth so full of living words. . . . O Thou aspect of graciousness to the saints, how very blessed is he who is found worthy of Thy sweet espousals.

Eternal Wisdom: Many are called to them, but few are chosen (p. 43).

This word of Eternal Wisdom, one remembers, is the conclusion of the parable of the vineyard,

which is so definite a part of the Pearl's discussion
on grace.   There follows further talk on the ineffable sweetness of God's love and the indifference
of many souls to it, in spirit and in figurative language entirely like *Pearl*.   As for instance:

The Servant: Now, then, my only elected Comforter,
speak one little word to my soul . . . for, lo! I am softly
asleep beneath Thy shadow, and my heart watcheth.
Eternal Wisdom: Listen, then, my son . . . enter
wholly into thy interior, and forget thyself and all things.
All the heavenly host follow Me entranced by new wonders and behold Me; their eyes are fixed on Mine; their
hearts are inclined to Me . . . My beloved ones are
encompassed by My love. (pp. 51-53)

The entire description of the loveliness and the
joy of the blessed corresponds in detail with
stanzas xciv, xcvi, of the poem, parts of which
have already been quoted in an earlier section of this chapter.   The Servant, like the poet,
is blessed with the gift of interrogation and asks
his vision pointedly the meaning of interior desolation; he wishes to know how a *loving* God can
withdraw Himself so completely from a soul.
This is the answer he receives:

Eternal Wisdom: In nothing canst thou discern My
presence so well as in this, namely, when I hide and
withdraw Myself from the soul, as not till then art thou

capable of perceiving who I am or what thou art. . . .
If ever thou art sensible of Me, enter into Thyself and
learn to separate the roses from the thorns, and to choose
out the flowers from the grass. [The same language of
grass and flowers that one finds in the poet's loss of his
pearl.]

The Servant: Lord . . . when my soul is deserted,
she is like a sick person who can relish nothing; who is
disgusted with everything; . . . dryness within, and
sadness without [an exact description of the disconsolate
poet]. But, Lord, when in the midst of my soul the
bright morning star arises, all my sorrow passes away, all
my darkness is scattered . . . then rejoices my soul, then
is my marriage feast. What before was hard . . . and
impossible, becomes easy and pleasant. . . . My soul is
then overflowed with clearness, truth, and sweetness, so
that she forgets all her toil.

. . . . . .

Eternal Wisdom: If . . . thou canst not endure My
absence with pleasure, wait for Me at least with patience. . . .

The Servant: O Lord, long waiting is painful.

Eternal Wisdom: He who will needs have love in
time, must know how to bear weal and woe. . . . What
is it thy soul seeks in exterior things who carries within
herself so secretly the kingdom of heaven?

The Servant: What is the kingdom of heaven, O
Lord, which is in the soul? [Identically the poet's question, "What is the peace that bearest as token this spotless pearl?"]

Eternal Wisdom: It is righteousness, and peace, and
joy in the Holy Ghost (pp. 61-64).

Here are all the conspicuous themes of *Pearl*: interior sadness, desolation, and explanation of these uses of adversity, the vision of heaven, the definition of spiritual peace. Here are likewise all the devices of *Pearl*: a transcendent Vision, dialogue, figures of grass and flowers, of jewels, of espousals and marriage feasts. Here are those other inevitable elements of spiritual autobiography so delicately used in *Pearl*: the Passion of Christ, and the Blessed Virgin. Whatever superficial resemblances the *Pearl* may bear to elegiac poetry, such complete and perfect parallels to it are assuredly lacking. Its place among spiritual autobiographies can hardly be more conclusively proved.

CHAPTER V

CONCLUSIONS

In calling the *Pearl* a spiritual autobiography, a complete study in spiritual dryness, from its acute attack to its entire cure, I realize that I have set at naught a tradition of a half a century and the judgment of eminent scholars as to the interpretation of the poem. That interpretation rests, as I have said before, entirely on assumption; the assumption that the poet was married, that he had a daughter, that this daughter died at the age of two, that he mourned for her at her grave. And, as I have said before, there is no reference to the poet's marriage in the poem; the talk is all of virginity as far as states of life are concerned. There is no mention of a daughter; the dream child is called a child only once; she is called "a maid of grace," a "maiden," "that Sweet," a "Pearl," a "damosel," "my bliss," "my bale," "Queen," "Bride," "that Gentle," "Brightest," "Lady," "my Precious," a wide and charming variety of quaint, sweet pet-names, to be sure; but not once "daughter" or "baby" or "my child." It seems unthinkable that a poet who could order his epithets to express so many subtle degrees of possession and tenderness would not once assert his paternity through them.

There is, throughout the poem, no mention of death, except as a natural phenomenon, common to all, and robbed of its sting by the death of Christ, and by His promise of resurrection to mankind. Above all, there is no reference to death in the opening stanzas where the pearl is lost. The gem slips "through grass to ground"; and the expectation that sweet spices and flowers will spring from that spot admits more easily of a spiritual than a natural interpretation.

Moreover, the spot where the poet mourned his pearl is expressly not a graveyard; it is an arbor shadowed with herbs, powdered with peonies, beauteous and bright with ginger, gromwell, and gilly flowers. It is the typical monastery garden, provided for even now by religious rule,[91] and used as a symbol in Suso's *Book of Eternal Wisdom.*

How many a precious spice garden is there . . . where lilies and roses formerly grew (p. 49).

---

[91] "Fragrant herbs, as thyme, summer savory, marjoram, etc., should be planted around the doors and windows." *Rules of the Sisters of the Holy Cross,* Notre Dame, Indiana, 1895, p. 151.

There are, indeed, several passages in the poem which seem to indicate the death of a child, but these have equal application to conditions common and familiar in religious life. On the other hand, there are numerous passages in *Pearl* which have no elegiac application, at all, and which clearly must be interpreted as depicting states of soul. The poem as a whole would yield no consolation to a bereaved father, but bears the most intimate significance to a religious. Above all, the heaven it describes is that of virgins, which has direct application to religious, but no bearing on a dead child or its father.

As a spiritual autobiography, the *Pearl* is perfectly true to type. It corresponds in technic and in content to the numerous spiritual classics of its kind. As a picture of interior desolation it is realistically accurate, as quotations have illustrated. In its climax and conclusion, in its definition of spiritual peace, and in the ultimate means of possessing this, the poem is entirely orthodox. Professor B. P. Kurtz has called it a "little Divine Comedy"; not less enthusiastic in my admiration, I shall be less comprehensive in my comparison. I think that the *Pearl* is a miniature "Paradiso" of the religious state, presenting a perfectly consistent exposition, revelation, and ecstatic climax of spiritual "blues."

BIBLIOGRAPHY

English Editions of the *Pearl*

MORRIS, RICHARD. *Early English Alliterative Poems.* London: 1864. Revised and reprinted 1869, 1885, 1896, 1901.

GOLLANCZ, ISRAEL. *Pearl, an English Poem of the Fourteenth Century.* Edited with Modern Rendering. London: 1891.

GOLLANCZ, ISRAEL. *Pearl,* edited with Modern Rendering together with Boccaccio's *Olympia.* London: 1921.

GOLLANCZ, ISRAEL. *Pearl, Cleanness, Patience* and *Sir Gawain* reproduced in facsimile from the unique ms. Cotton Nero A.X. in British Museum. Oxford: 1923.

COULTON, G. G. *Pearl.* Rendered into Modern English, a line for line version in meter of the original. London: 1906.

OSGOOD, C. G. *Pearl* (Belles Lettres Series). London: 1906.

MITCHELL, WEIR. *Pearl.* Metrical rendering of first half of poem. New York: 1906.

OSGOOD, C. G. *Pearl.* Prose translation. Princeton: 1907.

JEWETT, S. *Pearl.* Rendering in original meter. New York: 1908.

MEAD, M. *Pearl*—an English Vision-Poem of the Fourteenth Century, done into Modern Verse. Portland, Maine: 1908.

WESTON, J. L. *Pearl*. In "Romance, Vision and Satire" (a modified form of the original meter). 1912.

NEILSON, W. A. and WEBSTER, K. G. T. *Pearl*, in "Chief British Poets." Prose translation. Boston: 1916.

KIRTLAN, E. J. B. *Pearl*, a poem of Consolation. In modern English verse. London: 1918.

Works of General Reference on *Pearl*

TEN BRINK. *Early English Literature*. London: 1883.

TEN BRINK. *History of English Literature*, 1. New York: 1889.

BALDWIN, C. S. *English Mediæval Literature*. New York: 1914.

Cambridge History of English Literature, 1. Cambridge: 1908.

CHAMBERS, W. and R. *Encyclopedia of English Literature*, 1. London: 1903.

COURTHOPE, W. J. *History of English Poetry*, 1. New York: 1895.

Encyclopedia Britannica (11th Edition). *Pearl*.

GARNETT and GOSSE. *History of English Literature*, 1. New York: 1903.

JUSSERAND, J. J. *Literary History of the English People*, 1. New York: 1895.

SCHOFIELD, W. H. *History of English Literature—Norman Conquest to Chaucer*. Macmillan, 1906.

WELLS, J. E. *Manual of the Writings in Middle English*. New Haven: 1916. Also Supplements I and II.

Studies and Criticisms of *Pearl*

BATES, K. L. *The Dial.* Dec. 16, 1908, p. 450 ff.

BRADLEY, H. *The Academy,* July-December, 1890, 38, pp. 201, 249.

BROWN, C. F. "The Author of the 'Pearl' considered in the Light of His Theological Opinions," *Publications of the Modern Language Association.* XIX, pp. 114-154.

BROWN, C. F. "The Pearl, an Interpretation," *Modern Language Notes,* 34; pp. 42-43.

COOK, A. S. "Pearl" *Modern Philology,* October, 1908, pp. 196-200.

COULTON, G. G. "In Defense of Pearl," *Modern Language Review.* II, pp. 39-43.

GOLLANCZ, I. *The Academy.* 40, pp. 36, 116; 38, p. 223.

GARRETT, R. M. "The Pearl" *University of Washington Publications.* IV, pp. 1-45.

EMERSON, O. F. "Some Notes on Pearl," *Publications of the Modern Language Association.* XXXVII, pp. 52-93.

HULL, EMILY. *Pearl* as an expression of the art and the embodiment of the ideals of the Middle Ages—Master's Thesis at University of California. 1889 (2661).

KOLBING, E. *Englische Studien.* 16, pp. 268-273.

MORRIS, R. *The Academy.* 39, p. 602; 40, p. 76.

MORRIS, R. "An Old English Miscellany," *Early English Text Society.* London: 1872; p. 49.

MORRIS, R. *Early Eng. Allit. Poems* in West Midland Dialect of the fourteenth century. E. E. T. S. 1864*ff.*

NORTHUP, C. S. "Study of Metrical Structure of the *Pearl.*" *Publications of the Modern Language Association.* XII, pp. 326-340.

NORTHUP, C. S. *Journal of English and Germanic Philology.* 20, p. 288.

SCHOFIELD, W. H. "Symbolism, Allegory, and Autobiography in *The Pearl.*" *Publications of the Modern Language Association.* XXIV, pp. 585-675.

SCHOFIELD, W. H. "The Nature and Fabric of the Pearl," *Publications of the Modern Language Association.* XLX, pp. 154-215.

SEGAR, MARY. "Alexandria and the Mystical Writings of the Middle Ages," *Catholic World.* August, 1924, vol. 119, p. 639.

FLETCHER. "The Allegory of the Pearl." *Journal of English and Germanic Philology.* 20, p. 1.

TRAUTMANN, M. "Der Dichter Huchown und Seine Werke," *Anglia.* I, p. 109.

Related Studies in Spiritual Biography

Ancren, Riwle. Edited and translated from the semi-Saxon MS. of the thirteenth century by James Norton. London: 1853. English edition by Abbott Gasquet, St. Louis.

ST. ANGELIA OF FOLIGNO. In *Catholic Mysticism,* Algar Thorold. London: 1900.

ST. AUGUSTINE. *Confessions.* Everyman edition.

ST. BERNARD. *The Book of St. Bernard on the Love of God.* London.

ST. CATHERINE OF SIENA. *Dialogues.* Translated from the original Italian by Algar Thorold. London: 1907.

Cloud of Unknowing. Edited by E. Underhill.

St. Gertrude. *Life and Revelations.* London.

Hilton, Walter. *Scale of Perfection.* London: 1817.

Julian of Norwich. *Revelations of Divine Love.* London: 1923.

Kempis, Thomas à. *De Imitatione Christe.* Earliest English translations of the first three books. Edited by John H. Ingram. London: 1893.

Lull, Ramon. *The Book of the Lover and the Beloved.* New York: 1923.

Petersen, Gerlac. *The Fiery Soliloquy with God.* New York: 1921.

Rolle, Richard. *Fire of Love,* in English Prose Treatise of Richard Rolle Hample. London: 1866, 1921. Welsh Mystic (Iorwerth Dhu), *Dublin Review,* July, 1924.

Ruysbroeck, John. *Reflections from the Mirror of a Mystic.* Translated by E. Baillie. London: 1905.

Ruysbroeck, *Love's Gradatory.* Translated by Mother Jerome. New York.

Suso, Blessed Henry. *Life.* Written by himself. London.

Suso, Blessed Henry. *Little Book of Eternal Wisdom.* London, 1910.

Tauler, J. *Bekehrung.* Edited by Denifle, Strasburg: 1877.

Tauler, J. *Das Buch von der geistlichen Armut.* Edited by Denifle. Munich: 1877.

Welsh, Mystic. Iorwerth Dhu. *Dublin Review,* July, 1924.

Related Poetry

An English Miscellany. F. J. FURNIVALL. Oxford: 1901 (Quatrefoil of Love).
An Old English Miscellany. Early English Text Society. J. M. COOPER. London: 1871.
Early English Poems. H. S. PANCOAST. New York: 1910.
Mediæval Anthology. M. G. SEGAR. New York: 1915.
Poems of William de Shoreham. THOMAS WRIGHT. London: 1849.
Political, Religious and Love Poems (Quia Amore Langueo). F. J. FURNIVALL. London: 1903.
Some Minor Poems of the Middle Ages. M. G. SEGAR and E. PAXTON. New York: 1917.
Religious Pieces. Early English Texts Society.
The Vision of William Concerning Piers the Plowman. WILLIAM LANGLAND. Version by the author about 1377, edited by W. W. Skeat. Oxford: 1888.

General References

ALLETZ. *Dictionnaire Portatif des Conciles.* Paris: 1758.
AQUINAS, ST. THOMAS. *On Prayer and the Contemplative Life.* Taken from *Summa.* Translated by the Reverend Hugh Pope.
ST. BENEDICT. *The Rule of.* Translated by Cardinal Gasquet. London: 1909.
ST. BERNARD. *Works.* Translated, Eales and Hodges. London: 1889.
DOCTORIS SERAPHICA, ST. BONAVENTURAE. *Opera Omnia.* VIII. Quaracchi: 1882-1900.

BONAVENTURA, GIOVANNI DI. *Opera Omnia,* VIII, XII. Paris: 1864.

Bassuet, Œuvres de, II. Paris: 1845.

ST. CATHERINE OF SIENA. *Life,* by the Blessed Raymond Capua, her confessor. Translated from the French. Philadelphia: 1859.

GARDNER, EDMUND. *St. Catherine of Siena.* London: 1907.

Letters of St. Catherine of Siena. Translated and edited by Vida D. Scudder. New York: 1911.

Catholic Encyclopedia, I.

COOPER, C. H. *Memoir of Margaret of Richmond.* Cambridge: 1874.

CUTHBERT, BUTLER, DOM. *Western Mysticism.* London: 1922.

DE WULF. *Histoire de la Philosophie Médiévale.* Louvain: 1905.

DINNIS, ENID. *Anchorhold.* New York.

Encyclopedia Britannica. Ed. 11, vol. XXI.

FENELON. *Selections,* edited by J. R. G. Hassard. New York: 1864.

FONK, LEOPOLD, S. J. *The Parables of the Gospel.* New York: 1915.

ST. FRANCIS DE SALES. *Treatise on the Love of God.* London: 1884.

GASQUET, ABBOT. *English Monastic Life.* London: 1910.

GASQUET, ABBOT. *Monastic Life in the Middle Ages.* London: 1910.

HARE, W. L. *Mysticism of East and West.* London: 1923.

HAUREAU, J. B. *Hugues de St. Victor et l'edition de ses œuvres.* Paris: 1859.

HAUREAU, J. B. *Les Œuvres de Hugues de Saint Victor, essai critique*. Paris: 1886.

HEFELE. *Concillien Geschichte*. V. Freiburg: 1886.

HODGSON, G. *English Mystics*. Milwaukee: 1922.

HUGEL, BARON F. VON. *St. Catherine of Genoa*. London.

INGE, W. R. *Studies of English Mystics*. London: 1906.

INGE, W. R. *Christian Mysticism*. London: 1899.

INGE, W. R. *The Philosophy of Plotinus*. London: 1918.

JAMES, W. *Varieties of Religious Experience*. London: 1902.

JOLY, H. *Psychology of the Saints*. London: 1898.

JONES, R. *Studies in Mystical Religion*. New York: 1909.

KEMPIS, THOMAS à. *Sermons to Novices Regular*. Translated by Dom Vincent Scully, C. R. L. London: 1907.

LEHEN DE FATHER, S. J. *The Way of Interior Peace*. New York: 1870.

LOUISMET, DOM S. *Mystical Initiation*. New York: 1923.

MYREC, JOHN. *Instructions for Parish Priests*. Edited by E. Peacock. London: 1868.

Paradise or Garden of the Holy Fathers. Translated out of the Syriac by Earnest A. W. Budge. London: 1907.

POST-NICENE FATHERS. VI, IX, X. P. Schaff. New York: 1909.

ROLLE, RICHARD. *The Form of Perfect Living*. Modern English by G. E. Hodgson. London: 1910.

ROLLE, RICHARD. *English Prose Treatises*. Edited from

R. Thornton's MS. cir. 1440 by G. G. Perry. Early English Text Society. Edited by Horstmann.

SPURGEON, C. F. E. *Mysticism in English Literature.* Cambridge: 1913.

STEINER, R. *Mystics of the Renaissance.* New York: 1911.

STÖCKL. *Geschichte der Philosophie des Mittelalters,* II. Maintz: 1865.

SWEET. *Oldest English Texts.*

ST. TERESA. *Autobiography.* Edited by J. J. Burke. New York: 1911.

TERTULLIAN. *Opera,* II, IV. Leipsic: 1837.

TURNER, W. *History of Philosophy.* Boston: 1905.

UNDERHILL, E. *Mysticism.* London: 1911.

UNDERHILL, E. *The Mystic Way.* New York: 1914.

UNDERHILL, E. *The Essentials of Mysticism.* London: 1920.

WAITE, A. C. *Lamps of Western Mysticism.* London: 1923.

WATKINS, E. I. *The Philosophy of Mysticism.* New York: 1920.

INDEX

(1)